Quilled Christmas

Quilled Christmas

30 FESTIVE PAPER PROJECTS

Alli Bartkowski

LARK
New York

New York

An Imprint of Sterling Publishing Co., Inc.
1166 Avenue of the Americas
New York, NY 10036

ISBN 978-1-4547-1038-7

Distributed in Canada by Sterling Publishing Co., Inc.
c/o Canadian Manda Group, 664 Annette Street
Toronto, Ontario M6S 2C8, Canada
Distributed in the United Kingdom by GMC Distribution Services
Castle Place, 166 High Street, Lewes, East Sussex BN7 1XU, England
Distributed in Australia by NewSouth Books
45 Beach Street, Coogee, NSW 2034, Australia

For information about custom editions, special sales, and premium
and corporate purchases, please contact Sterling Special Sales at
800-805-5489 or specialsales@sterlingpublishing.com.

Manufactured in China

4 6 8 10 9 7 5 3

sterlingpublishing.com
larkcrafts.com

Interior design by Karla Baker
Cover design by David Ter-Avanesyan
Interior and cover photography by Chris Bain

Contents

Introduction

Christmastime is one of my favorite holiday seasons. In the fall, I begin quilling snowflakes for teachers, coaches, friends, and family. They are some of my favorite gifts to give, especially when they're attached to a bag of chocolates. Any quilled Christmas ornament is a guaranteed crowd-pleaser, and the receiver always cherishes it.

But in this book, I wanted to stretch my quilling knowledge beyond ornaments. I started to think about what home décor items I would love to proudly display when family and friends visit my home. As I worked on each project idea, I became more excited for the season to come! The projects include framed wall art to hang in your foyer in December, centerpieces to display on a kitchen table, and unique cards to make for that perfect hand-delivered present. I even have some jewelry projects you can wear to your annual festive holiday gatherings.

I also asked myself how I could combine old and new quilling techniques in this book. I love to use typical text-weight quilling paper. It makes intricate quilled shapes and the perfect off-center circle. But with the growing popularity of quillography and linear art, how could I combine these trends with basic quilling techniques? Linear art and quillography, which blends paper quilling and typography, became popular when graphic designers started using strips of paper in advertisements to add an element of dimension to their work. They would use card-stock strips like a paintbrush or marker to make pictures, outlines, or shading effects. The strips were also shaped into letters to highlight the words in the ads. Their thickness and stiffness makes it more difficult to roll them into loose or tight circles, but these qualities help create beautiful linear art and defined borders. After much experimentation, I created projects that showcase the best use of both types of paper. I love how well they complement each other when you use them along with crimping, banding, and lettering techniques.

This book is filled with Christmas projects of all different levels. If you're looking for a project using the basic quilled shapes in a simple pattern, then try the Easy level projects. For those who want to venture into new quilling techniques, go for a Medium project. Advanced quillers can definitely dive into the more intricate and difficult Hard projects, where you can master multiple techniques. There's something for everyone!

Quilling Basics

These unique Christmas projects only require some quilling tools and holiday-colored quilling papers. You'll enjoy learning a handful of new techniques and practicing some popular ones too.

Materials

To find quilling tools and papers, visit your large craft store chains. They may not always carry every color of paper, but they will have the basic quilling tools and variety packs to get you started. Online stores offer the best selection of quilling papers and card-stock strips for your projects. They will also have a good selection of tools to help with the techniques in this book.

Paper

Quilling paper comes in all lengths, widths, and weights; most of the projects in this book use text-weight quilling paper (70 lb. text or 105 gsm). You'll find that text-weight paper is the easiest to roll, mold, and shape. For quillography, you'll use special quillography strips that are often made of card stock (80 lb. cover or 190 gsm). They are stiffer to work with, but they are great for lines or borders. You'll see how you can combine both weights of paper to create beautiful quilled art projects.

Greeting cards work best with ⅛-inch (3 mm) wide paper. Miniature figures and three-dimensional projects are best made with a combination of ⅛-inch-wide (3 mm)

and ¼-inch-wide (6 mm) paper strips. The most difficult size to work with is the ¹⁄₁₆-inch (1.6 mm) width because the strip is very narrow and takes more practice to roll. However, it's best for adding small details, like buttons or faces. For the smaller projects, like the gift tags and

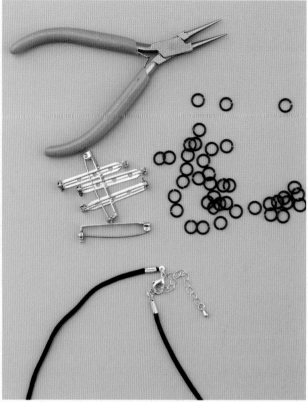

Festive Place-Card Holders (page 30), you can cut your own paper strips by hand with a paper cutter. For the larger projects, like the Hanging Christmas Wreath (page 62) or Manger Scene (page 66), precut papers are a better choice. Cutting papers by hand will be very time-consuming, and the resulting strips may be uneven. A paper shredder can speed up the process, but the strip will have rough edges, which may not look appealing. The benefits of using precut strips are smooth edges, uniform widths, and longer strip lengths. The convenient packaging also gives you a place to store and keep the quilling paper in good condition.

Embellishments

Only a few projects use embellishments to add sparkle or color. A rhinestone on a snowflake can be eye-catching. Ink pads can change the look of a plain piece of card stock, while chalk is useful for giving your Nutcracker (page 76) rosy cheeks. Add a special greeting to your cards and tags by using stamps or rub-on letters. Metallic cording is a functional tool that not only helps hold an ornament but also adds a finishing touch to a project. Visit your local craft stores to find all of these supplies.

Jewelry Findings

Some of the projects, like the Poinsettia Pin (page 91), can be turned into wearable art! Your local craft store will carry the pin backings and corded necklaces that you'll use to create some unique holiday jewelry.

Tools

The basic quilling tools help you quickly roll your paper. They are inexpensive and can be found in your local craft store or in an online quilling store.

slotted tool The slotted tool is designed to hold the paper's end so that you can immediately start rolling the paper. It's perfect for beginners and for rolling quilling shapes like loose circles, tight circles, and crimped strips.

needle tool This is basically a needle set into a handle. Rolling paper strips with this tool takes a little more practice than with the slotted tool, but most quillers prefer this one because it leaves a small, tight center that is more pleasing to the eye. It's also used for placing small amounts of glue on the paper strips.

Basic Quilling Tool Kit

- Slotted tool
- Needle tool
- Fine-tipped tweezers
- Toothpicks
- Scissors
- Ruler
- Straight pins
- Wax paper
- Corkboard or foam board
- Circle Template Board or Circle Sizer ruler
- Paper cutting tools (hole punch, paper trimmer, paper cutter, craft knife)
- Craft glue
- Sticky notepad

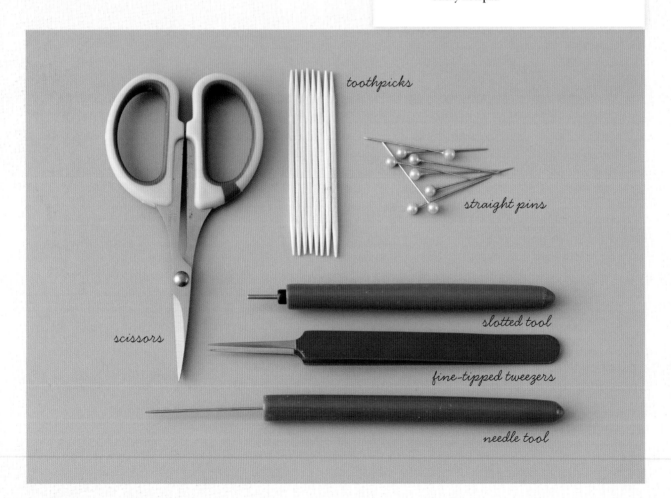

toothpicks

straight pins

slotted tool

fine-tipped tweezers

needle tool

scissors

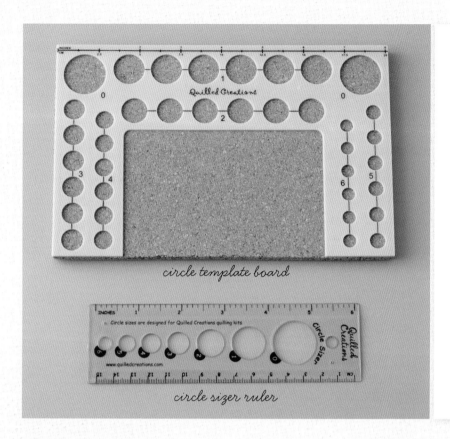

circle template board

circle sizer ruler

Circle Template Sizes

Size	Circle Diameter
0	1 inch (2.5 cm)
1	¾ inch (1.9 cm)
2	⅝ inch (1.6 cm)
3	½ inch (1.3 cm)
4	⁷⁄₁₆ inch (1.1 cm)
5	⅜ inch (9 mm)
6	⁵⁄₁₆ inch (7 mm)

fine-tipped tweezers Tweezers with small, pointed tips are essential for quilling and handling small pieces.

toothpicks Toothpicks are useful for placing glue on paper strips.

scissors Scissors with a fine tip are used for hand-fringing and trimming ends.

ruler A ruler is helpful for measuring your paper strips to size.

straight pins Straight pins are used to hold your quilled shapes together while piecing your project. They are also needed for the off-center circles technique (see page 17).

wax paper Use wax paper over your template to protect it from glue.

corkboard or foam board The corkboard or foam-board surface and straight pins are used to hold the quilled pieces together.

circle template board or circle sizer ruler A snowflake must have uniform pieces for it to be symmetrical. Using either of these tools is important because the instructions for most projects specify circle sizes to achieve a consistent quilled shape. These are also useful for off-center circles. In projects that include the Circle Template Board (CTB), a CTB number will be indicated to show you which circle template size to follow. Circle sizes are listed above.

paper cutting tools For card projects, you will need a paper trimmer. Most trimmers also have a scoring blade for making folds in card stock. For the "Joy" Pennant Banner (page 33), a handheld hole punch is used to create a hole in card stock, which will enable you to feed string to hang your banner pieces. Use a craft knife for cutting out letters from your card stock.

wax paper

sticky notepad

craft glue

corkboard

craft glue In quilling, you only need small dabs of glue to hold your circles together, since you are gluing paper to paper. Choose a liquid or water-based glue that dries clear. Avoid overly tacky glues that are hard to remove from your fingers and tools; these can slow you down and ruin the quilled shapes.

fine-tip glue bottle This glue bottle has a metal tip to dispense the glue as a fine line. It's very helpful when gluing strips onto a background for the quillography technique (see page 23).

sticky notepad A notepad is a convenient tool for holding a puddle of glue or cleaning off your needle tool. When the glue puddle dries, simply peel away the paper for a new, clean surface.

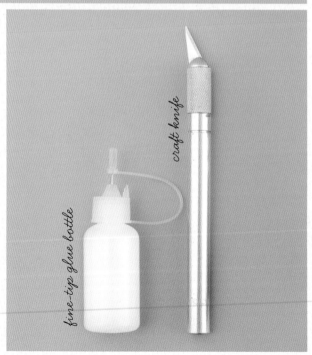

craft knife

fine-tip glue bottle

Technique Tools

combing tool The combing tool forms a strip of paper into evenly spaced loops. The numbered pins help track your looping pattern so that it's fast and easy.

mini mold This tool is wonderful for shaping tight circles into perfect domes and other three-dimensional shapes, such as dishes and flattop cones. If you don't have a Mini Mold, you can use small wooden balls instead.

curling coach The Curling Coach is used with the slotted tool. It holds and rolls the paper strips when using the "tuck and roll" technique (see page 19). It helps you roll strips with uniform finger pressure so that the tight circles can be shaped into large tight circles and domes.

border tools The Border Buddy makes paper rings to fill with quilling shapes or beehive curls. It comes in three different shapes: circle, square, and triangle. If you don't have a Border Buddy, you can use dowels of different diameters as a substitute. For larger circles, a few projects use cookie cutters with 1½-inch (3.8 cm), 2-inch (5.1 cm), and 2½-inch (6.4 cm) diameters.

crimper A crimper is a great way to add texture to your coils. Place the paper strip between the gear teeth and turn the knob to roll the paper strip.

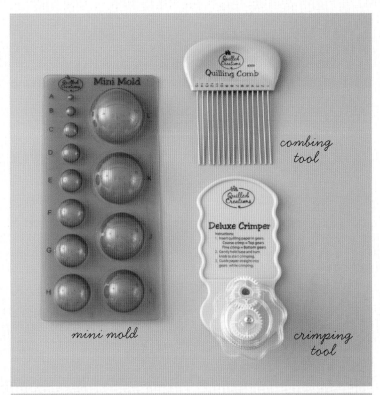

combing tool

mini mold

crimping tool

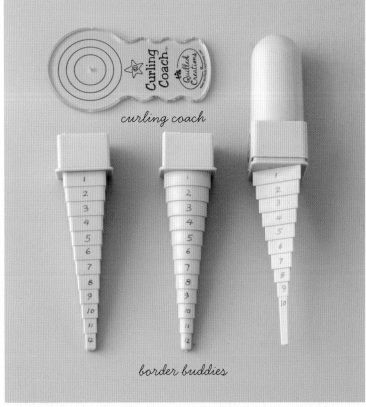

curling coach

border buddies

Quilling Techniques

ROLLING WITH A SLOTTED TOOL

1 Insert the end of the paper into the slot from the top (**a**).

2 Begin rolling the paper strip around the tip by rotating the tool in either direction (**b**).

3 To keep the coil's center from being pulled out, remove the coil by pushing from behind or underneath instead of pulling it off (**c**).

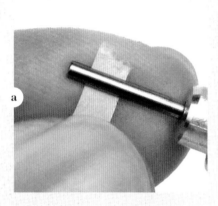

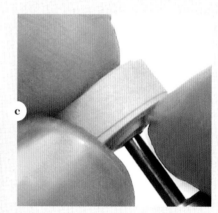

ROLLING WITH A NEEDLE TOOL

1 Scratch the end of the paper with your nail to soften the paper fibers. This will make it easier to wrap the paper end around the needle tip. You can also moisten the end of the paper strip so that it sticks to the needle when you are ready to roll it. Lay the needle on top of the end of the paper strip (**d**).

2 To start the roll, squeeze the end of the paper around the needle and roll it between your fingers without rotating the needle tool. The roll will start forming once the paper end is tucked under itself (**e**).

3 Continue to use light pressure, rolling the paper around the needle tool by moving your thumb and finger in opposite directions.

4 Slide the circle off the needle tool.

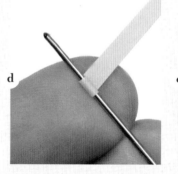

Tip

Tear quilling strips to the desired length instead of cutting them. The torn feathered end leaves a less obvious seam after gluing.

Gluing Basics

A corkboard or foam board surface and pins will help keep the wax paper and template in place. Also use pins to hold the pieces together as you follow the template pattern and glue assemblages together. A sticky notepad is great for holding a small puddle of glue. Use the needle tool to pick up a small amount of glue and spread the glue to close your circles. Spread the glue while joining pieces together to keep excess from squeezing out or dirtying the pieces.

ATTACHING END-TO-END

1 To roll two different-colored strips of paper, first align the two strips against a straight edge. Then place a dab of glue on the end of one of the strips (**f**).

2 Overlap the ends of two paper strips by ⅛-inch (3 mm) and glue them together (**g**).

3 Select the color for the center and start rolling from that end of the paper strip (**h**).

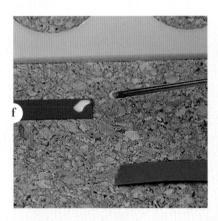

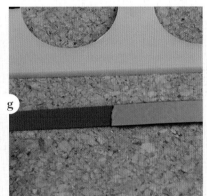

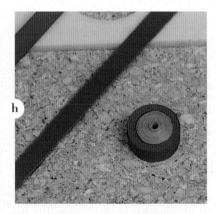

The combing tool makes evenly spaced loops fast! If you don't have the combing tool, then creating the same look is just as easy by hand.

LOOPING BY COMBING

A quilling combing tool has a handle with numbered prongs. It makes evenly spaced loops and consistently shaped pieces.

1 Make a small fold in the paper strip at pin #1. Place glue at the fold. Wrap the strip of paper around pin #2 and back up around pin #1 (**j**).

2 Move the strip between pins #3 and #4 (**k**).

3 Wrap the paper around pins #3 and #1 and glue at pin #1. Then continue making larger loops, gluing after each one, until you have the desired size (**l**).

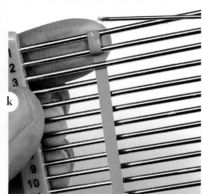
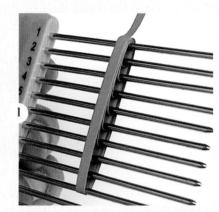

LOOPING BY HAND

1 Make a small loop with the paper strip. Wrap the paper around the end and make another loop that is slightly larger (**m**).

2 Continue making larger loops until you've reached the end of the paper strip.

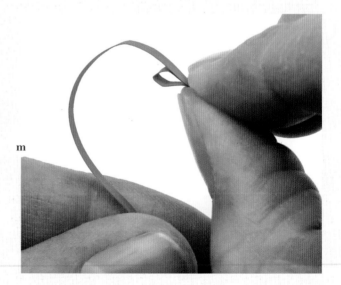

OFF-CENTER CIRCLE

1 Roll a paper strip and place the loose circle on a corkboard or in a Circle Template Board.

2 Pin the center of the circle to one side.

3 Use tweezers to even out the circle.

4 Spread a thin layer of glue over the paper edges between the pins, and let it dry (**i**).

5 To remove the pin, first twist the pin to break any glue sealed to it. Next pull the pin straight out.

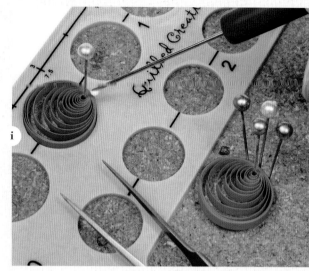

BORDER

1 Wrap a paper strip around a border tool (such as a Border Buddy or a cookie cutter) and glue after the first loop (**n**).

2 Wrap the rest of the paper length around the tool and carefully slide the loops off the tool (**o**).

3 Pull on the end to tighten the border shape and glue the end in place (**p**).

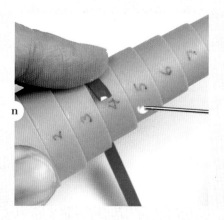
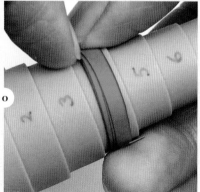
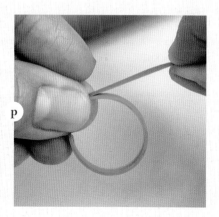

BEEHIVE SWIRLS

1 Place the slotted tool about ½ inch (1.3 cm) down from the end of the paper (**q**).

2 Roll the paper about ½ inch (1.3 cm) and remove the strip from the tool to see the swirl (**r**).

3 Insert the paper strip back into the tool about ½ inch (1.3 cm) down from the first swirl and roll the strip again. Remove from the tool and repeat (**s**).

4 Continue making beehive swirls down the entire length of the paper (**t**).

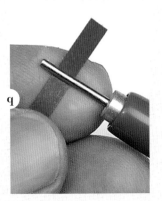  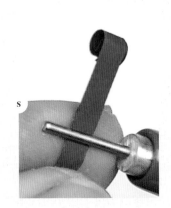 

CRIMPING

1 Insert a paper strip between the gears of a crimper (**u**).

2 Turn the knob or gears to crimp the entire length of the paper.

3 Use a slotted tool to roll the paper strip (**v**). Avoid flattening the crimps by holding the paper edge while rolling.

LARGE TIGHT CIRCLE: TUCK AND ROLL

1 Insert the slotted tool into the Curling Coach, then insert the strip of paper into the slot.

2 While rolling gently, place your finger at the side and your thumb on top of the circle. *Note. Do not press or wind the paper strip too tightly. Otherwise, it will be difficult to shape three-dimensional domes and cones (x).*

3 After rolling the first strip, leave the tail or end of the paper straight out. Tuck in the next strip of paper and continue winding the paper strip around the roll. As the circle gets larger, leave a longer "tail length." (The recommended tail length is three times the diameter of the rolled paper.) Continue rolling until you have the desired size, then glue the end in place (y).

4 To separate the large tight circle from the tool, rest the rolled paper and tool upside down on a flat surface. Pull the slotted tool straight out (z).

Tip

After rolling a large tight circle, place the circle on a hard, flat surface. To even out the paper edges, use the handle of the tool and roll on top of the tight circle. This helps prepare the circle for shaping.

DOME

1. After rolling a tight circle, select a dome size and hold the center of the tight circle against the top of the dome (**aa**).

2. Starting from the center of the circle, gently press down to start shaping the dome (**bb**).

3. Move both fingers outward to mold the rolled paper into a dome (**cc**).

4. To hold the shape, spread a thin layer of glue on the inside of the dome. Let it dry overnight.

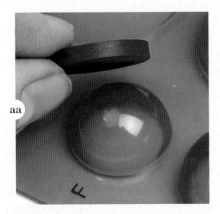
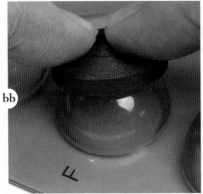
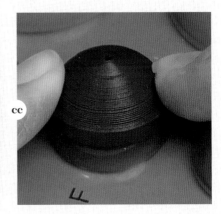

CONE

1. Shape the large tight circle into a dome. Hold the dome in your hand and squeeze the outer portion of the cone (**dd**).

2. Gently roll and squeeze the cone between your fingers as if you were turning a doorknob. You will start to see the layers of the circle slowly shift and form into a cone (**ee**).

3. Continue adding gentle pressure until you reach the desired cone shape (**ff**).

4. To hold the shape, spread a thin layer of glue on the inside of the cone. Let it dry overnight.

Tip

To redo the cone shape, flatten the cone completely. Shift the layers back and forth (inward and outward) a few times to even out the edges, then make a new dome with the Mini Mold.

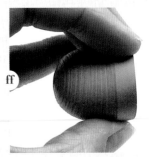

FLATTOP CONE

1   Shape the piece into a cone. Hold the wall of the cone on opposite sides with the thumb and forefinger of both hands. Tap the tip of the cone onto a flat surface. The layers will flatten based on how deep your fingers are holding the inside cone wall. For a flattop cone, place your fingers halfway into the cone (**gg**).

2   To hold the shape, spread a thin layer of glue on the inside of the flattop cone. Let it dry overnight.

DISH

1   Shape the large tight circle into a dome. Hold the wall of the dome on opposite sides with the thumb and forefinger of both hands. Place your remaining fingers near the top of the cone. Tap the dome's tip onto a flat surface. The layers will flatten near your fingertips (**hh**).

2   To hold the shape, spread a thin layer of glue on the inside of the dish. Let it dry overnight.

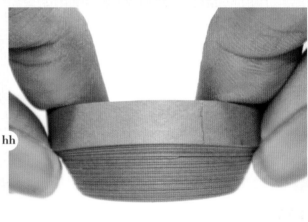

GLUING BACK SIDES FOR A FREESTANDING PIECE

After making large tight circles, wrapped assemblies, or loose circles, use your finger to spread a thin layer of glue on the back side of the piece so it doesn't come loose or pop out (**ii**). For loose circles, also spread a thin layer of glue along the ends. Avoid using too much glue at the center of the circle because the wetness of the glue can cause the circles to expand. Let the piece dry completely so the paper will stiffen and become more durable.

MULTILAYERED SCROLL

1 Stack three strips of the same length and glue the ends of the strips together (**jj**).

2 Roll the strip with a needle tool starting at the glued end (**kk**).

3 Unravel the scroll until the circle is your desired size. With your fingers, reroll to add more space between the circle and its center (**ll**).

4 Evenly separate each layer in the unraveled section by pulling on the end of each strip (**mm**).

5 Glue the ends together at the location where the shortest strip of paper ends (**nn**).

6 Trim off the excess strips of paper near where you've glued the ends together (**oo**).

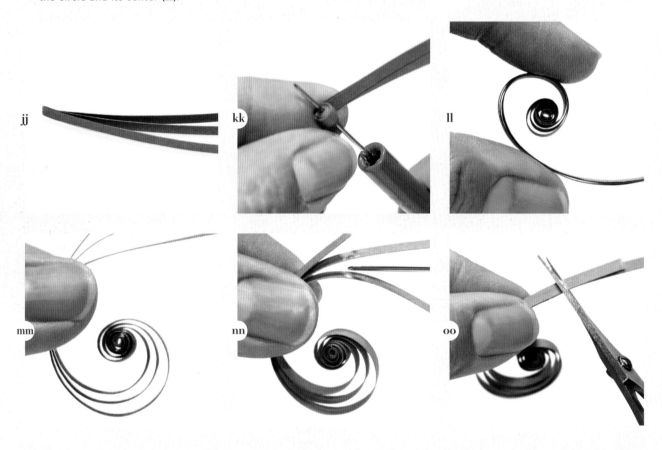

BANDING

1 Start with a straight, full-length strip of paper. Glue the "banding" strip at a 45° angle at one end.

2 Wrap the banding strip down the strip until you have reached the end of the banding strip (**pp**).

3 Glue the banding strip to the straight strip. Trim as desired and glue the banding ends at both ends so that it doesn't unravel.

pp

QUILLOGRAPHY

Quillography or card-stock strips are stiffer and easier to use for linear paper art, especially when you need to make straight or gently curved lines. It's helpful to work in small sections at a time. When outlining a shape or letter, trim the strip at a bend or a break in the design. Keep your hands and tools clean by frequently removing any glue residue from the tips of your fingers and tools.

1 Make a photocopy of the template. Flip the photocopy over and, on the back of the paper, rub pencil lead over the template lines (**qq**).

2 Align the template over your background with the lead rubbing facing down. Trace over the template with a pencil to make a faint line on your background (**rr**).

3 Working in small sections, hold the paper strips along the pencil line to measure and shape the paper strip. Make an indent in the strip of paper with tweezers to indicate where a transition or bend in the strip takes place. To make gentle curves in the paper strip, use your fingers and fingernails. Shape the strip to match the pencil line and trim after a few bends. Then use a fine-tip glue bottle to make a thin line over the pencil line (**ss**).

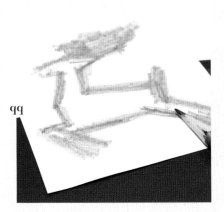

qq

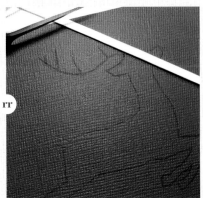

rr

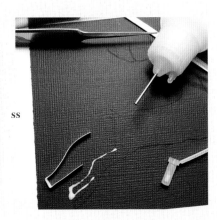

ss

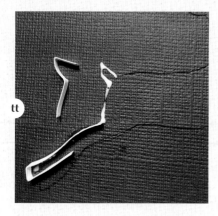
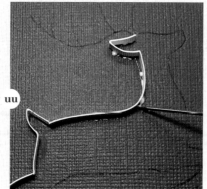
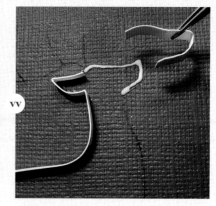

4 Carefully place the strip on the glue line. Then work on the next section of the line drawing (**tt**).

5 Use your needle tool to remove any excess glue. Because most craft glues will dry clear, this step may not always be necessary (**uu**).

6 Repeat this process section by section (**vv**).

7 When finished, set your piece aside to dry.

Tip

With card-stock strips, it's hard to create tight bends and curls without the paper layers coming apart. Soften the strip's fibers by rubbing the strip between your fingers and the needle tool in both directions, then try making the small bends and curls.

CUTTING NARROW STRIPS

To cut a 1/16-inch-wide (1.6 mm) strip of paper, use fine-tip scissors to cut a 1/8-inch-wide (3 mm) paper strip in half lengthwise. Hold the paper strip in one hand and the scissors in the other. Cut toward the center of the strip, watching the tip of the scissors—not the scissor blades—as you move along the strip. By watching the tip of the scissors, you will guide the cutting direction more accurately and always cut down the middle (**xx**).

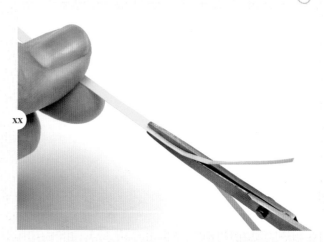

Basic Quilled Shapes

tight circle Roll the paper strip until you've reached the end. Glue the end to the roll to prevent the circle from expanding open. Use the handle of the slotted or needle tool to press down on the paper edges to even them out.

loose circle Roll the paper strip as you did with the tight circle. Remove the circle from the tool and let it unravel open. Place a small dab of glue on the loose end and press it against the circle.

teardrop/curved teardrop Roll a loose circle and simply pinch a point on the circle. To evenly pinch each layer, shift the center of the circle to one side and then pinch a point. For a curved teardrop, use your fingernail or the tip of the slotted tool to curve the point.

marquise/curved marquise Starting with a loose circle, use both hands to pinch points at opposite sides of the circle at the same time. For a curved marquise, use your fingernail or the tip of the slotted tool to curve the points.

half circle/flat half circle Start with a teardrop and pinch a second point near the first point. For a flat half circle, pinch the second point farther away from the first point until one of the edges is straight.

crescent Roll a loose circle. Pinch a half circle with the two points farther apart.

triangle Start with a teardrop shape and press the rounded end inward to form two additional points.

heart Holding the point of a teardrop, use your fingernail to press in the rounded end to make the curves and the indentation on the top of a heart.

arrow Holding most of a teardrop, use your finger to press on the rounded end to make a small indentation and two new points.

square/diamond Roll a marquise. Turn the piece 90° and pinch two more points opposite each other.

rectangle/parallelogram Roll a marquise. Turn the piece slightly and pinch two more points opposite each other.

star Start with a diamond shape. Hold the points and press the sides inward, then push the points together to make two more points on each side.

holly leaf Roll a rectangle. Pinch two more points opposite each other. Pinch each point again and curve the sides inward.

tight oval/egg Roll a tight circle. Pinch it flat into an oval or with a point to make an egg shape. Use the handle of a tool to press down and even out the paper strip's edges. Release the circle just slightly to make it easier to shape the piece.

tight/loose circle Roll the paper strip into a tight circle. Remove it from the tool and let it expand slightly open between your fingers or in a circle template. Place a small dab of glue on the loose end, and press it against the circle. This shape can be pinched into a teardrop.

Basic Quilled Scrolls

loose scroll Roll a paper strip at one end. Leave the other end loose or unglued.

s-scroll Roll half a paper strip. Roll the other end of the paper strip in the opposite direction.

v-scroll Fold the strip in half. Roll the ends of the paper strip either in the same direction or in different directions.

y-scroll Fold the paper strip in half crosswise. Glue the strip together near the fold. Roll the ends outward.

c-scroll Roll half of the paper strip, then, at the other end, roll the paper strip in the same direction.

swooping scroll Roll a loose scroll and then unravel part of the scroll. Gently reroll the unraveled part, making the circles farther apart.

double scroll Fold the strip of paper in half crosswise. Starting from the fold, roll the paper strip into a swooping scroll. Shift one layer of the paper slightly and glue the loose ends together. Trim the end with scissors.

Basic Quilled Shapes

tight circle

loose circle

teardrop/curved teardrop

marquise/curved marquise

half circle/flat half circle

crescent

triangles

heart

arrow

square/diamond

rectangle/parallelogram

star

holly leaf

tight oval/egg

tight/loose circle

Basic Quilled Scrolls

loose scroll

s-scroll

v-scroll & variation

y-scroll

c-scroll

swooping scroll

double scroll

Home Décor

Festive
PLACE-CARD HOLDERS

Complete your Christmas dinner table with these unique place-card holders for your special guests.

easy

1" × 2½" × 3"
(2.5 × 6.4 × 7.6 cm)

What You Need

Basic Quilling Tool Kit (page 10)

Template

Quilling paper, ¼ inch (6 mm) wide:
beige

Quilling paper, ⅛ inch (3 mm) wide:
leaf green, yellow, raspberry, metallic
silver, white, red, teal, metallic gold

Card stock: white

Ink pen

Quilling Shapes

tight circle   *loose circle*   *square*   *marquise*

triangle   *star*   *teardrop*   *half circle*

rectangle   *flat half circle*

Techniques

Attaching End-to-End (page 15)

Off-Center Circles (page 17)

What You Do

1   Lay the template between the corkboard and a sheet of wax paper.

2   Make bases for the four place-card holders. For each base, glue six 16-inch (40.6 cm) lengths of beige quilling paper together using the end-to-end technique. Roll the entire strip to make a tight circle.

3   Make the Christmas tree place-card holder. Roll a 16-inch (40.6 cm) length of leaf-green quilling paper into a flat half circle (CTB size 1). For the middle of the tree, roll a 12-inch (30.5 cm) length of leaf-green quilling paper into a flat half circle (CTB size 2). For the tree's top, roll an 8-inch (20.3 cm) length of leaf-green quilling paper into a triangle (CTB size 3). For the star, roll a 4-inch (10.2 cm) length of yellow quilling paper into a star (CTB size 6). Glue the star and the top, middle, and bottom of the tree together as shown in the template. Repeat to make the other tree. Glue the two trees on the base about ¹⁄₁₆ inch (1.6 mm) apart.

4   Make the ornament place-card holder. Roll a 16-inch (40.6 cm) length of raspberry quilling paper into a loose off-center circle (CTB size 1). For the top of the ornament, roll a 6-inch (15.2 cm) length of silver quilling paper into a rectangle (CTB size 6). Using scissors, cut a small ¾-inch (1.9 cm) length of silver quilling paper to create the loop for the top of the ornament. Glue the pieces together as shown in the template. Repeat to make the other ornament. Glue the two ornaments to the base about ¹⁄₁₆ inch (1.6 mm) apart.

5   Make the candy cane place-card holder. Roll three 6-inch (15.2 cm) lengths of red quilling paper into loose circles. Pinch one circle into a teardrop, one into a half circle, and one into a marquise (CTB size 5). Roll three 6-inch (15.2 cm) lengths of white quilling paper into loose circles (CTB size 5). Pinch one into a half circle, one into a marquise, and one into a triangle. Glue the pieces together to make the candy cane as shown in the template. Repeat to make the other candy cane. Glue the two candy canes to the base about ¹⁄₁₆ inch (1.6 mm) apart.

Circle Templates

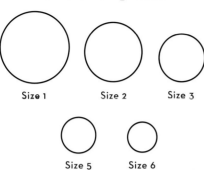

Size 1 Size 2 Size 3

Size 5 Size 6

6 Make the gift box place-card holder. Roll a 16-inch (40.6 cm) length of teal quilling paper into a square (CTB size 1). Using scissors, cut a small piece of gold paper to make the ribbon on the side of the gift box. Glue the ribbon in place. For the bow, roll two 4-inch (10.2 cm) lengths of gold quilling paper each into teardrops (CTB size 6). Glue the bow on top of the gift box. Repeat to make the other gift box. Glue the two gift boxes to the base about $1/16$ inch (1.6 mm) apart.

7 Cut four $2\frac{1}{2} \times 3$–inch (6.4 × 7.6 cm) rectangles from the white card stock. Write names onto the pieces of paper and insert them into the place-card holders.

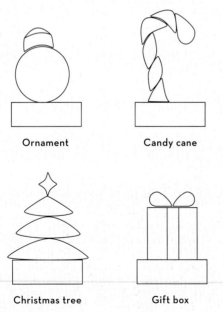

Ornament   Candy cane

Christmas tree   Gift box

"Joy"
PENNANT BANNER

Welcome your family and friends with a banner that will catch their eyes. Quillography is a great way to customize a banner to capture the spirit of Christmas.

What You Need

Basic Quilling Tool Kit (page 10)

Card stock: light brown

Template

Pencil

Quillography paper, ⅛ inch (3 mm)
wide: forest green

Quilling paper, ⅛ inch (3 mm) wide:
sage green, red

Hole punch

Cording: gold

Quilling Shapes

holly leaf *tight circle*

Technique

Quillography (page 23)

Circle Template

Size 1

What You Do

1   Cut out five triangles with a base of 4 inches (10.2 cm)
and a height of 5 inches (12.7 cm) from the light-brown
card stock.

2   Using the template and the pencil, trace the letters *J*, *O*,
and *Y* onto three of the triangles.

3   With forest-green quillography paper, form each letter
with the quillography technique. Determine where to
start each section of the letter using the directions and
arrows in the template.

4   Make 13 holly leaves. For each holly leaf, roll a 16-inch
(40.6 cm) length of sage-green quilling paper into a holly
leaf shape (CTB size 1). You will need one leaf for each
letter and 10 leaves for the two endpieces.

5   Make 15 berries. To make the berries, roll an 8-inch
(20.3 cm) length of red quilling paper into a tight circle
for each one. You will need three berries for each letter
and six berries for the endpieces.

6   For the three triangles with letters, glue a holly leaf and
three berries to each letter as shown in the template.

7   For the endpieces, glue five holly leaves into a star
shape, using the template as a reference. Glue three
berries to the center.

8   Using the hole punch, punch a small hole in each upper
corner of the triangle pieces. Cut a piece of cord
approximately 50 inches (1.3 m) long. Run the gold
cording through the holes of each triangle and use
the cording to hang your banner.

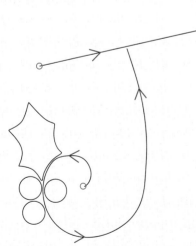

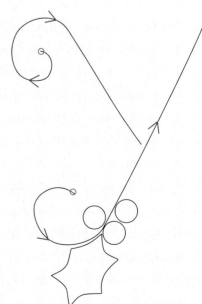

"Noel"
LIGHT DISPLAY

Whether it's day or night, place this sign in
a spot where it will greet guests.

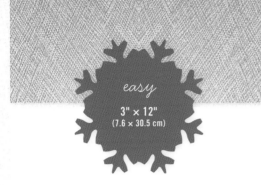

easy

3" × 12"
(7.6 × 30.5 cm)

What You Need

Basic Quilling Tool Kit (page 10)

Card stock: black

Pencil

Template

Translucent vellum paper: white

Double-sided tape or tape runner

Quilling paper, ⅛ inch (3 mm) wide:
white

Quilling paper, ¼ inch (6 mm) wide:
metallic gold

4 battery-operated tea lights

Quilling Shapes

*swooping
scroll*   *tight circle*   *curved
marquise*   *marquise*

arrow   *diamond*   *y-scroll*

Technique

Banding (page 23)

Circle Templates

Size 1   Size 2

Size 3   Size 5

What You Do

1 Cut out a 3 × 12-inch (7.6 × 20.3 cm) rectangle from the black card stock.

2 To space out the letters evenly, mark a line every 3 inches (7.6 cm) across the black card stock with a pencil to make four 3-inch (7.6 cm) squares. Using the template, trace the letters on the card stock at the center of each square and cut the letters out with a craft knife.

3 Cut out four 3-inch (7.6 cm) squares from the translucent paper. Attach each square to the black card stock with double-sided tape or a tape runner.

4 For the letter *N*, roll seven 4-inch (10.2 cm) lengths of white quilling paper each into a curved marquise (CTB size 5) and twelve 4-inch (10.2 cm) lengths of white quilling paper each into a swooping scroll. Glue "the marquises and scrolls on the back of the translucent paper.

5 For the letter *O*, make a snowflake. For the center of the snowflake, roll six 12-inch (30.5 cm) lengths of white quilling paper each into a large diamond (CTB size 2) and glue the ends of the diamonds together. Roll six 8-inch (20.3 cm) lengths of white quilling paper each into a small diamond (CTB size 3). Glue the small diamond between the points of the large diamonds and then glue the entire snowflake to the back of the translucent paper.

6 For the letter *E*, roll six 8-inch (20.3 cm) lengths of white quilling paper each into a curved marquise (CTB size 3) and nine 4-inch (10.2 cm) lengths of paper each into a Y-scroll. Arrange three Y-scrolls and two marquises on each arm of the *E*. Glue the pieces to the back of the translucent paper.

7 For the letter *L*, roll three 16-inch (40.6 cm) lengths of white quilling paper each into a marquise (CTB size 1), a 4-inch (10.2 cm) length of white quilling paper into a tight circle, two 4-inch (10.2 cm) lengths of white quilling paper each into a swooping scroll, and four 8-inch (20.3 cm) lengths of white quilling paper each into an arrow (CTB size 3). First, glue the tight circle to the bottom corner of the letter on the back of the translucent paper. Next, glue the marquises together and then glue this piece to the back of the translucent paper. The ends of the marquise piece should touch the tight circle. Glue one swooping scroll and two arrows on each arm of the letter on the back of the translucent paper.

8   To make the top border on the front of the light display, cut two 16-inch (40.6 cm) lengths of gold quilling paper. Band one gold strip around the other at a 45° angle. Trim and glue a 12-inch (30.5 cm) length of the banded strip on the top of the piece. Repeat to make the bottom border.

9   Tape a tea light behind each letter. The tea light will also serve as the base to hold the quilled piece.

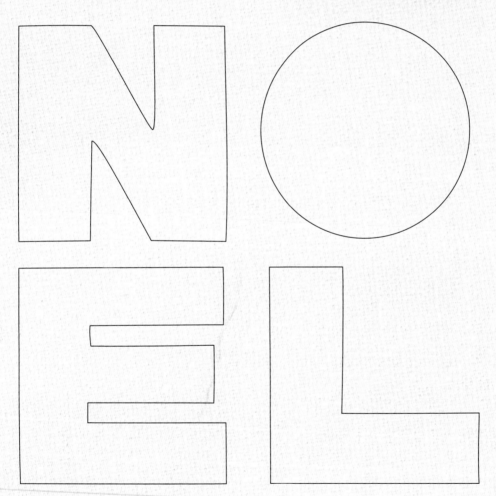

Mistletoe

SPRIG

Kissing under mistletoe is a European tradition. The mistletoe grants those who kiss beneath it strength, peace, health, fertility, and love!

medium

5" × 2"
(12.7 × 5.1 cm)

What You Need

Basic Quilling Tool Kit (page 10)

Template

Quilling paper, ⅛ inch (3 mm) wide:
sage green, moss green,
crimson, white

Mini Mold

String for hanging

Quilling Shapes

tight circle

flat half circle

arrow

loose circle

crescent

Techniques

Attaching End-to-End (page 15)

Dome (page 20)

Circle Template

Size 1

What You Do

1 Lay the template between the corkboard and a sheet of wax paper.

2 Make seven leaves. Roll eleven 16-inch (40.6 cm) lengths of sage-green quilling paper and three 16-inch (40.6 cm) lengths of moss-green quilling paper each into a flat half circle (CTB size 1). For each leaf, glue two half circles together.

3 Make seven stems. For each stem, cut an 8-inch (20.3 cm) length of sage-green quilling paper. To attach the stems, wrap each length around a leaf and glue the loose ends together.

4 Group all of the leaves together as shown in the photo. Wrap a 4-inch (10.2 cm) length of crimson quilling paper around the stems.

5 Make the bow. Roll six 16-inch (40.6 cm) lengths of crimson quilling paper into loose circles (CTB size 1). Pinch four of the circles into crescents and two into long arrows. Glue two crescents and one arrow onto each side of the crimson paper wrapped around the stems.

6 Make seven berries. For each berry, use the end-to-end technique to glue a 1-inch (2.5 cm) length of moss-green quilling paper to an 8-inch (20.3 cm) length of white quilling paper. Starting from the moss-green end, roll the strip into a tight circle and shape it into a dome (Dome A). Glue the berries to the leaves using the template as a guide.

7 Tie a string around the stems to hang the mistletoe over a doorframe, or use it as a gift topper.

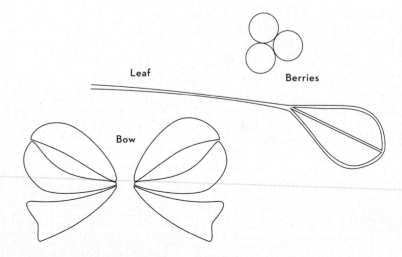

Leaf

Berries

Bow

Christmas Wreath
FRAMED ART

This wreath may look complicated to make, but all you have to do is repeat the same quarter section of teardrops three times. Hang this frame on your wall or place it on your dining table as a centerpiece for your guests to admire.

8" × 8"
(20.3 × 20.3 cm)

What You Need

Basic Quilling Tool Kit (page 10)

Card stock: white

Pencil

Template

Quillography paper, ⅛ inch (3 mm) wide: black, forest green

Quilling paper, ⅛ inch (3 mm) wide: forest green, sage green, leaf green, moss green, red

Frame, 8 × 8 inches (20.3 × 20.3 cm)

Quilling Shapes

curved teardrop

tight circle

Technique

Quillography (page 23)

Circle Templates

Size 1

Size 2

Size 3

Size 5

What You Do

1 Cut an 8-inch (20.3 cm) square from the white card stock.

2 With a pencil, trace *Merry Christmas* and the circular stem onto the white card stock.

3 Using the quillography techniques, bend, shape, and trim a black quillography strip to form the letters in *Merry Christmas*. Glue it onto the traced letters.

4 Outline the four branches. Use a 16-inch (40.6 cm) length of forest-green quillography paper for each branch. Trim each branch to the appropriate length as shown on the template.

5 Make 56 leaves for the branches. Each branch will have 14 leaves. For each leaf, roll curved teardrops with quilling paper. The size, colors, and quantity of each teardrop leaf are as follows:

COLOR	16 inches (40.6 cm) (CTB size 1)	12 inches (30.5 cm) (CTB size 2)	8 inches (20.3 cm) (CTB size 3)	6 inches (15.2 cm) (CTB size 5)
Forest Green	2	0	1	1
Sage Green	0	2	1	1
Leaf Green	0	1	1	1
Moss Green	1	0	1	1

6 Make eight large berries, 20 medium berries, and 16 small berries. For each large berry, roll an 8-inch (20.3 cm) length of red quilling paper into a tight circle. For each medium berry, roll a 4-inch (10.2 cm) length of red quilling paper into a tight circle. For each small berry, roll a 2-inch (5.1 cm) length of red quilling paper into a tight circle. Each branch will have two large berries, five medium berries, and four small berries.

7 Lay out the leaves and berries around the circular branches using the template as reference. Glue them to the white card stock.

8 Place the finished piece inside the frame.

Holiday Lights Tree

FRAMED ART

A rainbow of colors can make the holiday even brighter!
Here's a delightful way to create a Christmas tree to
complement your holiday décor.

medium

5" × 7"
(12.7 × 17.8 cm)

What You Need

Basic Quilling Tool Kit (page 10)

Template

Card stock: white

Quillography paper, ⅛ inch (3 mm)
wide: forest green

Quilling paper, ⅛ inch (3 mm) wide:
red, sunset, yellow, lime green, light
blue, pink, lilac, forest green

Frame, 5 × 7 inches (12.7 × 17.8 cm)

Quilling Shapes

teardrop   *tight circle*   *rectangle*

Technique

Quillography (page 23)

Circle Template

Size 6

What You Do

1 Trace the outline of the cord as shown in the template onto the white card stock.

2 Using the quillography technique, glue a forest-green quillography-paper strip on the outline of the tree. Trim the strip, using the template as a guide.

3 Make 35 light bulbs. Roll 4-inch (10.2 cm) lengths of the following strips each into a teardrop (CTB size 6):

- Five red lengths of quilling paper
- Five sunset-colored lengths of quilling paper
- Five yellow lengths of quilling paper
- Five lime-green lengths of quilling paper
- Five light-blue lengths of quilling paper
- Five pink lengths of quilling paper
- Five lilac lengths of quilling paper

4 Make 35 sockets for the light bulbs. For each socket, roll a 2-inch (5.1 cm) length of forest-green quilling paper into a tight circle.

5 Glue the sockets and light bulbs to the cord as shown in the photo on the previous page.

6 Make the plug. For the base, roll a 4-inch (10.2 cm) length of forest-green quilling paper into a rectangle. Glue it to the end of the cord. For the prongs, roll two ½-inch (1.3 cm) lengths of yellow quilling paper. Pinch to flatten them and glue them on top of the plug's base.

7 Place the piece inside the frame.

Santa & Reindeer
FRAMED ART

In this frame, capture a moment that happens every Christmas Eve: Santa with all his reindeer rushing through the night to deliver gifts!

8½" × 14"
(21.6 × 35.6 cm)

What You Need

Basic Quilling Tool Kit (page 10)

Card stock: dark blue

Quilling paper, ⅛ inch (3 mm) wide:
crimson, metallic gold, red, pale
peach, white, light brown, beige,
black

Template

Quillography paper, ⅛ inch (3 mm)
wide: white

Frame, 8½ × 14 inches
(21.6 × 35.6 cm)

Quilling Shapes

crescent   triangle   loose scroll   tight circle

half circle   marquise   teardrop   tight oval

loose circle   c-scroll   curved
teardrop

v-scroll   rectangle

Techniques

Looping (page 16)

Cutting Narrow Strips (page 24)

Quillography (page 23)

What You Do

1 Make the frame. Cut out a 6½ × 12-inch (16.5 × 30.5 cm) rectangle from the dark-blue card stock.

2 Make the body of the sleigh. Roll two 16-inch (40.6 cm) lengths of crimson quilling paper each into a crescent (CTB size 1) and a 6-inch (15.2 cm) length of crimson into a triangle (CTB size 5). Glue the crescents and triangle together as shown in the template. For the gold trim on top of the sleigh, loop a 16-inch (40.6 cm) length of gold quilling paper by hand to make a looped piece that is 2 inches (5.1 cm) in length. Bend and fold the looped piece to fit on top of the sleigh. For the gold trim on the front of the sleigh, roll a 2-inch (5.1 cm) length of gold quilling paper into a loose scroll and glue it into place.

3 Make the sleigh's runner. Roll two 1½-inch (3.8 cm) lengths of gold into tight circles. Set them aside. With a 3-inch (7.6 cm) length of gold quilling paper, roll the ends and leave about an inch (2.5 cm) of the strip's center straight. Glue the tight circles onto the straight section of the paper and then glue the entire runner to the bottom of the sleigh. Set the sleigh aside.

4 Make Santa's figure. For his body, roll a 16-inch (40.6 cm) length of red quilling paper into a half circle (CTB size 1). For his head, roll a 3-inch (7.6 cm) length of pale peach into a marquise. For the beard, roll a 4-inch (10.2 cm) length of white quilling paper into a teardrop (CTB size 6). For the mustache, roll a 1-inch (2.5 cm) length of white quilling paper into a tight oval. For his hat, roll a 6-inch (15.2 cm) length of red quilling paper into a triangle (CTB size 5) and a 2-inch (5.1 cm) length of white quilling paper into a rectangle. Glue all the pieces together using the template as reference.

5 For Santa's bag, roll an 8-inch (20.3 cm) length of white quilling paper into a half circle (CTB size 3), a 1-inch (2.5 cm) length of white quilling paper into a triangle, and a 1-inch (2.5 cm) length of gold quilling paper into a C-scroll. Glue the scroll and bag together. Then glue the bag to the sleigh and Santa.

Circle Templates

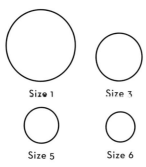

Size 1   Size 3

Size 5   Size 6

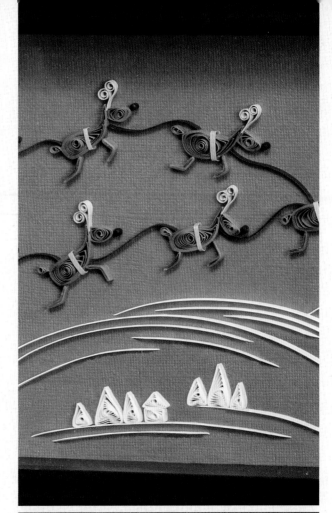

6 Make the nine reindeer. For the body of each reindeer, roll a 16-inch (40.6 cm) length of light-brown quilling paper into a curved teardrop (CTB size 1). For each head, roll a 4-inch (10.2 cm) length of light-brown quilling paper into a half circle (CTB size 6). Make two legs for each reindeer. For each leg, cut a 3-inch (7.6 cm) length of light-brown quilling paper. Make a fold ⅜ inch (9 mm) from the end of one strip and continue making ⅜-inch (9 mm) folds to form a thick, flat piece. Fold the piece in half to make the bend in the reindeer's leg. For the antlers, roll a 2-inch (5.1 cm) length of beige quilling paper into a V-scroll with the ends rolled in the same direction. For eight of the noses, roll a 1-inch (2.5 cm) length of black quilling paper into a tight circle. For the last nose, roll a 1-inch (2.5 cm) of red quilling paper into a tight circle. To assemble each reindeer, glue the body, head, antler, legs, and nose together. Use the red nose for the reindeer in the front to make Rudolph.

7 Make a harness for each reindeer. Cut a 6-inch (15.2 cm) length of gold quilling paper lengthwise to make two narrow strips. Trim the narrow strips into 1-inch (2.5 cm) lengths and glue one around each reindeer's body.

8 Make 12 pine trees. For the large pine trees, roll six 8-inch (20.3 cm) lengths of white quilling paper into triangles (CTB size 3). For the medium-sized pine trees, roll three 6-inch (15.2 cm) lengths of white quilling paper into triangles (CTB size 5). For the small pine trees, roll three 4-inch (10.2 cm) lengths of white quilling paper into triangles (CTB size 6).

9 Make two houses. Roll four 4-inch (10.2 cm) lengths of white quilling paper into loose circles (CTB size 6). Pinch two into rectangles and two into triangles. Glue a triangle and rectangle together. Set them aside.

10 Make the snowy hillsides. Trim the white quillography strips into the different lengths shown in the template and slightly curve each strip. The lengths of each strip can be any size. The template shows examples of how many strips you can use for each hillside and how to layer the strips. With scissors, round both ends of each strip.

11 Lay out Santa's sleigh and reindeers on the top half of the dark-blue card stock piece. For the rope, use 1½-inch (3.8 cm) lengths of crimson quilling paper and curl them slightly to connect the sleigh to the reindeer. Glue the pieces onto the dark-blue card stock.

12 To assemble the snowy mountain scene, lay out the hillsides, pine trees, and houses on the lower half of the dark blue card stock. Glue the pieces to the background.

13 Place the finished piece inside the frame.

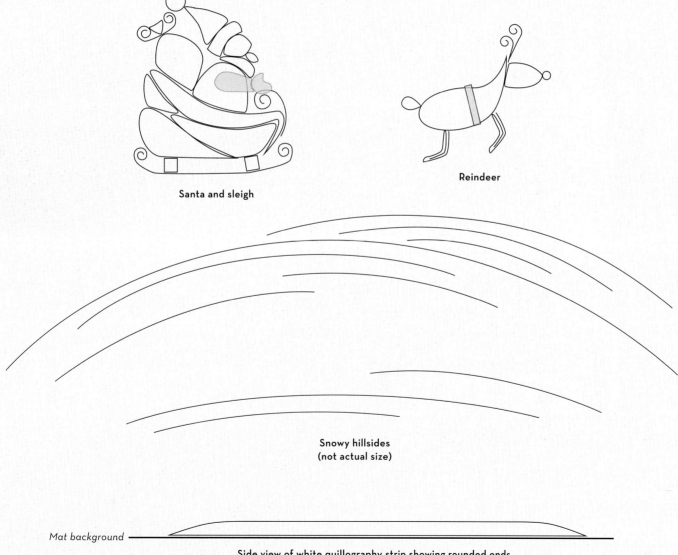

Santa and sleigh

Reindeer

Snowy hillsides
(not actual size)

Mat background

Side view of white quillography strip showing rounded ends

"Peace, Love, Joy"
FRAMED ART

A rainbow of colors can make the holiday even brighter!
Here's a delightful way to create a Christmas tree to
complement your holiday décor.

medium

8" × 8"
(20.3 × 20.3 cm)

What You Need

Basic Quilling Tool Kit (page 10)

Card stock: white

Template

Quillography paper, ⅛ inch (3 mm)
wide: crimson, white

Quilling paper, ⅛ inch (3 mm) wide:
sage green, crimson, white

Frame, 8 × 8 inches (20.3 × 20.3 cm)

Quilling Shapes

arrow *curved marquise* *marquise*

diamond *tight circle*

Technique

Quillography (page 23)

Circle Templates

Size 1 Size 3

Size 5 Size 6

What You Do

1 Cut an 8-inch (20.3 cm) square from the white card stock.

2 Transfer the template onto the white card stock.

3 Make the words. Use the quillography technique and 16-inch (40.6 cm) lengths of crimson quillography strips. Reference the template to determine where you should trim each strip. Glue the strips in place onto the card stock.

4 Make six large leaves. For each large leaf, roll a 4-inch (10.2 cm) length of sage-green quilling paper into a curved marquise (CTB size 6). Glue the leaves to the words.

5 Make six small leaves. For each small leaf, roll a 2-inch (5.1 cm) length of sage-green quilling paper into a curved marquise. Glue the leaves to the words, as shown in the template.

6 Make six berries. For each berry, roll a 2-inch (5.1 cm) length of crimson quilling paper into a tight circle. Glue the berries to the words, as shown in the template.

7 Make the large snowflake on the right side of the word *love*. For the snowflake's frame, cut three 3-inch (7.6 cm) lengths of white quillography strips. Fold each length in half crosswise. Glue the strips into place using the quillography technique and the template as reference. For the center of the snowflake, roll six 16-inch (40.6 cm) lengths of white quilling paper into diamond (CTB size 1). Glue the diamonds with their points facing the center. For the endpoints and the small branches on the snowflake's arms, cut twenty-four ¼-inch (6 mm) lengths of white quillography strips. Fold twelve of the lengths in half crosswise. Glue the folded and unfolded strips into place using the quillography technique and the template as reference. For the large branches on each arm of the snowflake, roll twelve 4-inch (10.2 cm) lengths of white quilling paper into marquises (CTB size 6). Glue the marquises below the snowflake's endpoints.

8 Make the medium snowflake on the right side of the word *joy*. For the snowflake's frame, cut three 2-inch (7.6 cm) lengths of white quillography strips. Fold each length in half crosswise. Glue the strips into place using the quillography technique and the template as reference. For the center, roll six 6-inch (15.2 cm) lengths of white quilling paper into arrows (CTB size 5). Glue the arrows between the glued quillography strips with their points facing away from the center. For the endpoints, cut twenty-four ¼-inch (6 mm) lengths of white quillography strips. Glue the strips into place using the quillography technique and the template as reference.

9 Make the medium snowflake on the left side of *joy*. For the snowflake's frame, cut three 2-inch (5.1 cm) lengths of white quillography strips. Fold each length in half crosswise. Glue the strips into place using the quillography technique and the template as reference. For the center of the snowflake, roll six 8-inch (20.3 cm) lengths of white quilling paper into arrows (CTB size 3) and six 4-inch (10.2 cm) lengths of white quilling paper into diamonds (CTB size 6). Glue the arrows between the glued quillography strips with their points facing the center. Glue the diamonds onto the arrows. For the endpoints, cut twenty-four ¼-inch (6 mm) lengths of white quillography strips. Glue the strips into place using the quillography technique and the template as reference.

10 Make the small snowflake above the word *peace*. For the snowflake's frame, cut three 1½-inch (3.8 cm) lengths of white quillography strips. Fold each length in half crosswise. Glue the strips into place using the quillography technique and the template as reference. For the center, roll six 8-inch (20.3 cm) lengths of white quilling paper into marquises (CTB size 3). Glue the marquises between the glued quillography strips with their points facing the center. For the endpoints, cut twenty-four ¼-inch (6 mm) lengths of white quillography strips. Fold twelve in half crosswise. Glue the unfolded and folded strips into place using the quillography technique and the template as reference. Roll six 2-inch (5.1 cm) lengths of white quilling paper into tight circles. Glue the tight circles to the ends of each snowflake's arm.

11 Make the small snowflake on the left side of *love*. For the snowflake's frame and center, cut three 1½-inch (3.8 cm) lengths, six ½-inch (1.3 cm) lengths, and six ¼-inch (6 mm) lengths of white quillography strips. Fold each length in half crosswise. Glue the strips into place using the quillography technique and the template as reference. For the endpoints, roll twelve 4-inch (10.2 cm) lengths of white quilling paper into marquises (CTB size 6). Glue the marquises to the snowflake's arms.

12 Place the finished piece inside the frame.

Christmas Tree
CENTERPIECE

Create this amazing centerpiece with ten stacked layers made from hundreds of quilled marquises. It's sure to be a topic of conversation during dinner.

hard

5½" × 5½" × 8½"
(14 × 14 × 21.6 cm)

What You Need

Basic Quilling Tool Kit (page 10)

Template

Quilling paper, ¼ inch (6 mm) wide:
leaf green

Quilling paper, ⅛ inch (3 mm) wide:
metallic gold, red

Ink pad: gold

Mini Mold

Quilling Shapes

marquise   *star*   *tight circle*

diamond   *tight-loose
circle*

Techniques

Gluing Back Sides
for a Freestanding Piece (page 21)

Cone (page 20)

Banding (page 23)

Dome (page 20)

Circle Templates

Size 1   Size 2

Size 3   Size 4

What You Do

1 Lay the template between the corkboard and a sheet of wax paper. If you prefer, you can make all the pieces at once using ¼-inch-wide (6 mm) leaf-green quilling paper. In total, you'll need:

- Two hundred 16-inch (40.6 cm) lengths rolled into marquises (CTB size 1)

- Sixty-four 12-inch (30.5 cm) lengths rolled into marquises (CTB size 2)

- Seventy-two 8-inch (20.3 cm) lengths rolled into marquises (CTB size 3)

- Eight 8-inch (20.3 cm) lengths rolled into marquises (CTB size 4).

- Two 8-inch (20.3 cm) lengths rolled into stars (CTB size 3).

2 For Layer 1, make eight branches. For each branch, roll five 16-inch (40 cm) lengths into marquises (CTB size 1). Glue the marquises for each branch together as shown in the template. Lay out the branches in a ring using the concentric circles on the template and glue them together. Spread glue onto the back of the layer. Let it dry completely.

3 Make eight standoffs between Layers 1 and 2. For each standoff, roll two 16-inch (40.6 cm) lengths into marquises (CTB size 1). Glue one marquise on top of the other. Space the standoffs evenly around the ring of branches and glue them into place.

4 For Layer 2 and the standoffs between Layers 2 and 3, repeat steps 2 and 3.

5 For Layer 3, make eight branches. For each branch, roll three 16-inch (40.6 cm) lengths into marquises (CTB size 1) and two 8-inch (20.3 cm) lengths into marquises (CTB size 3). Glue the marquises together as shown in the template. Lay out the branches in a ring using the circle template and glue them together. Spread glue onto the back of the layer. Let it dry completely.

6 Make four standoffs between Layers 3 and 4. For each standoff, roll two 16-inch (40.6 cm) lengths into marquises (CTB size 1). Glue one marquise on top of the other. Space the standoffs evenly around the ring of branches and glue them into place.

7 For Layer 4 and the standoffs between Layers 4 and 5, repeat steps 5 and 6.

8 For Layer 5, make eight branches. For each branch, roll three 16-inch (40.6 cm) lengths into marquises (CTB size 1). Glue the marquises together to make a branch as shown in the template. Lay out the branches in a ring using the circle template and glue them together. Spread glue onto the back of the layer. Let it dry completely.

9 Make four standoffs between Layers 5 and 6. For each standoff, roll two 12-inch (30.5 cm) lengths into marquises (CTB size 2). Glue one marquise on top of the other. Space the standoffs evenly around the ring of branches and glue them into place.

10 For Layer 6, make eight branches. For each branch, roll three 12-inch (30.5 cm) lengths into marquises (CTB size 2). Glue the marquises together as shown in the template. Lay out the branches in a ring using the circle template and glue them together. Spread glue onto the back of the layer. Let it dry completely.

11 Make four standoffs between Layers 6 and 7. For each standoff, roll two 12-inch (30.5 cm) lengths into marquises (CTB size 2). Glue one marquise on top of the other marquise. Space the standoffs evenly around the ring of branches and glue them into place.

Layers 3 & 4

Layer 5

Layer 6

Layers 1 & 2

Layer 7

Layer 9

Layer 8

Layer 10

Star/tree topper

12 For Layer 7, roll sixteen 12-inch (30.5 cm) lengths into marquises (CTB size 2). Using the template as a guide, glue eight marquises together to make a flower. Glue the other eight marquises between the petals. Spread glue onto the back of the layer. Let it dry completely.

13 Make four standoffs between Layers 7 and 8. For each standoff, roll two 8-inch (20.3 cm) lengths into marquises (CTB size 3). Glue one marquise on top of the other. Space the standoffs evenly around the ring of branches and glue them into place.

14 For Layer 8, roll eight 8-inch (20.3 cm) lengths into marquises (CTB size 3) and roll eight 12-inch (30.5 cm) lengths into marquises (CTB size 2). Glue the small marquises together to make a flower, as shown in the template. Glue the large marquises between the flower petals. Spread glue onto the back of the layer. Let it dry completely.

15 Make four standoffs between Layers 8 and 9. For each standoff, roll two 8-inch (20.3 cm) lengths into marquises (CTB size 3). Glue one marquise on top of the other. Space the standoffs evenly around the ring of branches and glue them into place.

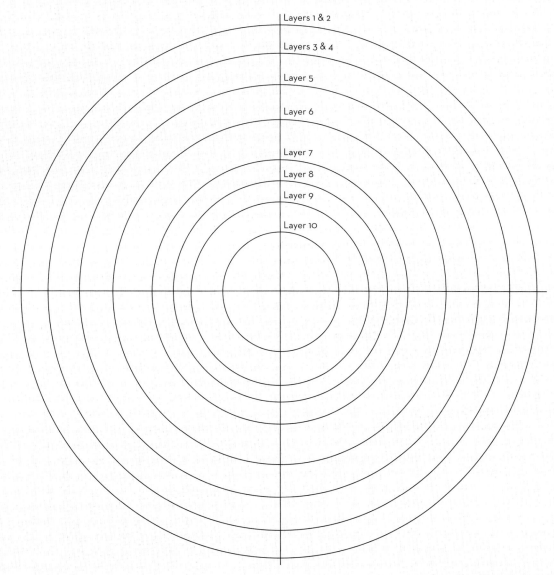

Layers 1 & 2
Layers 3 & 4
Layer 5
Layer 6
Layer 7
Layer 8
Layer 9
Layer 10

16 For Layer 9, roll sixteen 8-inch (20.3 cm) lengths into marquises (CTB size 3). Glue eight marquises together to make a flower, as shown in the template. Glue the remaining marquises between the flower petals. Spread glue onto the back of the layer. Let it dry completely.

17 Make one standoff between Layers 9 and 10. Roll an 8-inch (20.3 cm) length into a star shape (CTB size 3). Glue the star to the center of Layer 9.

18 For Layer 10, roll eight 8-inch (20.3 cm) lengths into marquises (CTB size 4). Glue the marquises together as shown in the template. Spread glue onto the back of the layer. Let it dry completely

19 Make one standoff between Layer 10 and the star of the Christmas tree. Roll an 8-inch (20.3 cm) length of leaf-green quilling paper into a star (CTB size 3). Glue the star to the center of Layer 9 and the other to the center of Layer 10.

20 For the star Christmas tree topper, roll five 16-inch (40.6 cm) lengths of gold quilling paper into tight/loose circles (CTB size 3). Pinch the circles into diamonds. Glue the diamonds together as shown in the template. Once the glue is dry, add gold ink to the edges or the star. Let the ink dry as well.

21 For the star's base, roll a 16-inch (40.6 cm) length of gold quilling paper into a cone. Spread glue on the inside of the cone and let it dry. Glue it to the star.

22 Assemble the tree. Glue each layer of the tree together, checking that the layers are centered and the points of each layer are offset. Glue the star on top of the standing on Layer 10. Use the diagram, opposite, for reference.

23 For the gold garland, make five banded strips. For each strip, use the banding technique to wrap a strip of gold quilling paper around three 16-inch (40.6 cm) lengths of gold quilling paper. This will add some stiffness to the garland. Gently curve and twist the garland before wrapping it around the tree. Glue the end of a banding strip between two leaves. Then glue the next banding strip near the previous banding strip and continue to wrap the garland around the tree.

24 To place the garland onto the tree, insert the end of the garland between the branches on Layer 1 and begin wrapping the garland around the tree. After you've used 4 to 5 inches (10.2 to 12.7 cm) of the garland, trim the banded strip and glue the trimmed end between the nearest branches. Continue gluing, wrapping, trimming, and gluing the garland until you reach the top of the tree.

25 Make 20 red ornaments. For each ornament, roll a 16-inch (40.6 cm) length of red quilling paper first into a tight circle and then into a dome (Dome B). Spread glue on the inside of the dome and let it dry. Glue four ornaments on every other layer of the tree, beginning on Layer 1.

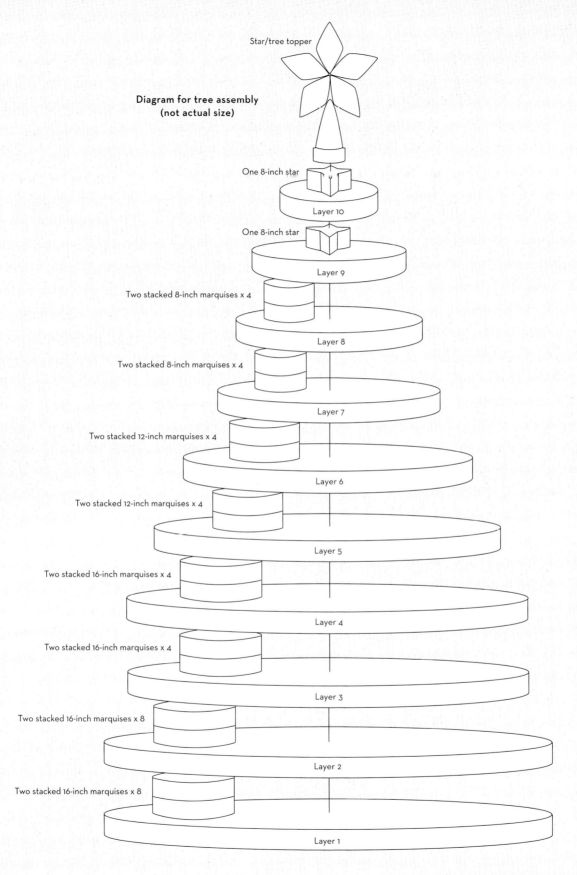

Star/tree topper

Diagram for tree assembly
(not actual size)

One 8-inch star

Layer 10

One 8-inch star

Layer 9

Two stacked 8-inch marquises x 4

Layer 8

Two stacked 8-inch marquises x 4

Layer 7

Two stacked 12-inch marquises x 4

Layer 6

Two stacked 12-inch marquises x 4

Layer 5

Two stacked 16-inch marquises x 4

Layer 4

Two stacked 16-inch marquises x 4

Layer 3

Two stacked 16-inch marquises x 8

Layer 2

Two stacked 16-inch marquises x 8

Layer 1

Hanging Christmas
WREATH

Get ready for the holiday season by creating your own
gorgeous wreath. The lilies add a beautiful pop of bright
white against the two-tone dark green leaves.

hard

8" × 8"
(20.3 × 20.3 cm)

What You Need

Basic Quilling Tool Kit (page 10)

Template

Quilling paper, ¼ inch (6 mm) wide:
forest green, sage green

Quilling paper, ⅛ inch (3 mm) wide:
white, moss green, sage green,
crimson

Mini Mold

Cording: silver

Quilling Shapes

marquise   *flat half circle*   *tight circle*

Techniques

**Gluing Back Sides
for a Freestanding Piece (page 21)**

Multilayered Scroll (page 22)

Dome (page 20)

Circle Templates

Size 1   Size 2

What You Do

1 Lay the template between the corkboard and a sheet of wax paper.

2 Make nine large forest-green leaves. For each leaf, roll five 16-inch (40.6 cm) lengths of forest-green quilling paper into marquises (CTB size 1). Glue them together as shown in the template. Wrap a 16-inch (40.6 cm) length of ¼-inch-wide (6 mm) forest-green quilling paper around each large leaf three times and trim the excess paper at the base of the leaf.

3 Make nine large forest-green/sage-green leaves. For each leaf, roll three 16-inch (40.6 cm) lengths of ¼-inch-wide (6 mm) forest-green quilling paper and two 16-inch (40.6 cm) lengths of ¼-inch-wide (6 mm) sage-green quilling paper into marquises (CTB size 1). Glue them together as shown in the template. You can randomly place the sage-green marquises. Wrap a 16-inch (40.6 cm) length of ¼-inch-wide (6 mm) forest-green quilling paper around each large leaf three times and trim the excess paper at the base of the leaf.

4 Make 11 small forest-green leaves. For each leaf, roll three 16-inch (40.6 cm) lengths of ¼-inch-wide (6 mm) forest-green quilling paper into marquises (CTB size 1). Glue them together to make a small leaf as shown in the template. Wrap an 8-inch (20.3 cm) length of ¼-inch-wide (6 mm) forest-green quilling paper around each small leaf twice and trim the excess paper at the base of the leaf.

5 Make 11 small forest-green/sage-green leaves. For each leaf, roll three 16-inch (40.6 cm) lengths of ¼-inch-wide (6 mm) forest-green quilling paper and one 16-inch (40.6 cm) length of ¼-inch-wide (6 mm) sage-green quilling paper into marquises (CTB size 1). Glue them together as shown in the template. You can randomly place the sage-green marquises. Wrap an 8-inch (20.3 cm) length of ¼-inch-wide (6 mm) forest-green quilling paper around each small leaf twice and trim the excess off at the base of the leaf.

6 Assemble the wreath. Using the template as a reference, lay out the leaves. Don't worry if the leaves do not fit exactly, since each leaf shape will differ slightly from the outlines in the template. For the outer ring of leaves, glue the large leaves together, alternating the solid forest-green leaves with the forest-green/sage-green large leaves. For the inner ring, glue the small leaves to the large leaves, alternating the solid forest-green leaves with the forest-green/sage-green small leaves. Spread a thin layer of glue over the back of the wreath. This will strengthen the entire wreath and help it hold its shape. Let it dry completely. Set the eight remaining small leaves aside.

7 Make two large lilies. For each lily, roll twelve 16-inch (40.6 cm) lengths of 1/8-inch-wide (3 mm) white quilling paper into flat half circles (CTB size 1). To make a petal, glue two half circles together. Repeat to make a total of six petals. Using the template as a reference, glue the petals into two groups of three. Stack the petal groups, and glue the layers together. For the centers, roll six 2-inch (5.1 cm) lengths of 1/8-inch-wide (3 mm) moss-green quilling paper into tight circles. Glue three circles on top of each flower.

8 Make one small lily. Roll twelve 12-inch (30.5 cm) lengths of 1/8-inch-wide (3 mm) white quilling paper into flat half circles (CTB size 2). To make a petal, glue two half circles together. Repeat to make a total of six petals. Using the template as a reference, glue the petals together into two groups of three. Stack the groups of petals and glue the layers together. For the centers, roll six 1-inch (2.5 cm) lengths of 1/8 inch-wide (3 mm) moss-green quilling paper into tight circles. Glue three circles on top of each flower.

9 Glue the eight small leaves, two large lilies, and one small lily around the wreath.

10 Make eight moss-green multilayered scrolls. For each scroll, roll three 4-inch (10.2 cm) lengths of moss-green quilling paper scrolls using the multilayered scroll technique. Repeat to make seven sage-green multi-layered scrolls.

11 Make 16 berries. For each berry, roll a 16-inch (40.6 cm) length of 1/8-inch-wide (3 mm) crimson quilling paper into a dome (Dome B).

12 Lay out the scrolls and berries randomly around the wreath. Glue the pieces onto the wreath.

13 Tie the silver cording to the top of the wreath for hanging.

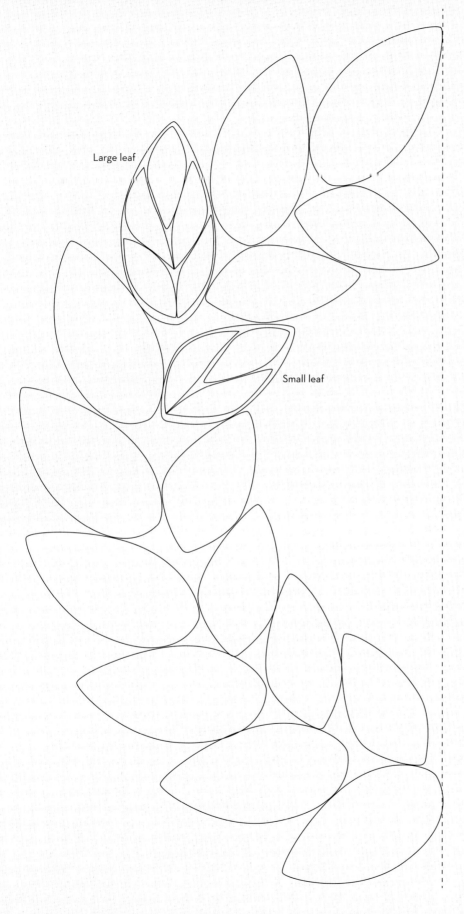

Large leaf

Small leaf

Lily (top and bottom petals)

Lily (center)

Manger Scene

Complete your Christmas decorating with this soon-to-be cherished nativity scene. It's truly a piece of art that will be passed down from generation to generation.

hard

2½" to 3" TALL
(6.4 to 7.6 cm)

What You Need

Basic Quilling Tool Kit (page 10)

Mini Mold

Quilling paper, ¼ inch (6 mm) wide: platinum white, golden, light blue, white, deep blue, brown, beige, forest green, light brown, royal blue, crimson,

Quilling paper, ⅛ inch (3 mm) wide: platinum white, pale peach, pale blue, metallic gold, brown, light brown, golden, white, forest green, metallic silver, royal blue, beige, light brown, crimson, black, sage green, dark gray, gray, ivory, pale pink

Border Buddy

Template

Quilling Shapes

tight circle

teardrop

loose scroll

loose circle

marquise

half circle

rectangle

Techniques

Dome (page 20)

Large Tight Circle: Tuck and Roll (page 19)

Cone (page 20)

Off-Center Circles (page 17)

Dish (page 21)

Attaching End-to-End (page 15)

Cutting Narrow Strips (page 24)

Flattop Cone (page 21)

Banding (page 23)

What You Do
Manger Scene

1   For the angel, make the following domes using the tuck and roll technique. Spread glue on the inside of the domes and let them dry.

  • For the body, roll four 16-inch (40.6 cm) lengths of ¼-inch-wide (6 mm) platinum-white quilling paper into a cone (Dome E).

  • Make two arms. For each arm, roll one 16-inch (40.6 cm) length of ⅛-inch-wide (3 mm) platinum-white quilling paper into a slightly curved cone (Dome B).

  • Make two hands. For each hand, roll one 16-inch (40.6 cm) length of ⅛-inch-wide (3 mm) pale-peach quilling paper into a dome (Dome B). Pinch it into a teardrop shape.

  • For the head, roll one 16-inch (40.6 cm) length of ⅛-inch-wide (3 mm) pale-peach quilling paper into a dome (Dome C).

  • For the hair, roll one 16-inch (40.6 cm) length of ¼-inch-wide (6 mm) golden quilling paper into a dome (Dome C).

2   Make the angel's wings. For each wing, roll a 16-inch (40.6 cm) length of ⅛-inch-wide (3 mm) platinum-white quilling paper into an off-center circle (CTB size 1). Pinch the circle into a teardrop.

3   Make the halo. Wrap a 4-inch (10.2 cm) length of ⅛-inch-wide (3 mm) metallic gold quilling paper around the Border Buddy tool (size 9).

4   Using the template as a guide, assemble the angel. Glue the arms, hands, and wings to the body. Glue the two halves of the head and hair together. Let them dry completely. Then glue the head onto the body and the halo onto the head.

5   For Mary, make the following domes using the tuck and roll technique. Spread glue on the inside of the domes and let them dry.

67

Circle Templates

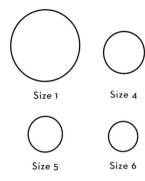

Size 1 Size 4

Size 5 Size 6

- For the body, roll four 16-inch (40.6 cm) lengths of ¼-inch-wide (6 mm) light-blue quilling paper into a cone (Dome E).

- Make two arms. For each arm, roll one 16-inch (40.6 cm) length of ⅛-inch-wide (3 mm) light-blue quilling paper into a slightly curved cone (Dome B).

- Make two hands. For each hand, roll one 16-inch (40.6 cm) length of ⅛-inch-wide (3 mm) pale-peach quilling paper into a dome (Dome B). Pinch it into a teardrop.

- For the head, roll one 16-inch (40.6 cm) length of ⅛-inch-wide (3 mm) pale-peach quilling paper into a dome (Dome C).

- For the hair, roll one 16-inch (40.6 cm) length of ⅛-inch-wide (3 mm) brown quilling paper into a dome (Dome C).

6 Make Mary's headscarf. Trim a 3-inch (7.6 cm) length of ¼-inch-wide (6 mm) white quilling paper and round two of the corners.

7 Using the template as a guide, assemble Mary. Glue the arms and hands to the body. Glue the two halves of the head and hair together. Let them dry completely. Then glue the head to the body and the headscarf to the head.

8 For Joseph, make the following domes using the tuck and roll technique. Spread glue on the inside of the domes and let them dry.

- For the body, roll four 16-inch (40.6 cm) lengths of ¼-inch-wide (6 mm) deep-blue quilling paper into a cone (Dome E).

- Make two arms. For each arm, roll one 16-inch (40.6 cm) length of ⅛-inch-wide (3 mm) light-brown quilling paper into a slightly curved cone.

- Make two hands. For each hand, roll one 16-inch (40.6 cm) length of ⅛-inch-wide (3 mm) pale-peach quilling paper into a dome (Dome B). Pinch it into a teardrop.

- For the head, roll one 16-inch (40.6 cm) length of ⅛-inch-wide (3 mm) pale-peach quilling paper into a dome (Dome C).

- For the hair, roll one 16-inch (40.6 cm) length of ⅛-inch-wide (3 mm) light-brown quilling paper into a dome (Dome C).

9 Make Joseph's headscarf. Cut a 1½-inch (3.8 cm) length of ¼-inch-wide (6 mm) brown quilling paper.

10 Using the template as a guide, assemble Joseph. Glue the arms and hands to the body. Glue the two halves of the head and hair together. Let them dry completely. Then glue the head to the body and the headscarf to the head.

11 For Baby Jesus, make the following domes using the tuck and roll technique. Spread glue on the inside the domes and let them dry.

- For the body, roll two 16-inch (40.6 cm) lengths of ⅛-inch-wide (3 mm) white quilling paper into a dome (Dome C).

- For the head, roll one 16-inch (40.6 cm) length of ⅛-inch-wide (3 mm) pale-peach quilling paper into a dome (Dome B).

12 Make the baby's halo. Wrap a 2-inch (5.1 cm) length of ⅛-inch-wide (3 mm) metallic-gold quilling paper around the round Border Buddy tool (size 12).

13 For the manger, roll six 16-inch (40.6 cm) lengths of ⅛-inch-wide (3 mm) brown quilling paper into a dish shape using the tuck and roll technique. Spread glue on the inside of the dish to hold its shape. For the legs beneath the manger, roll four 4-inch (10.2 cm) lengths of ⅛-inch-wide (3 mm) brown quilling paper into tight circles. Glue them to the bottom of the manger. For the straw, cut five 1-inch (2.5 cm) lengths of ¼-inch-wide (6 mm) golden quilling paper. Cut small fringes at both ends of each strip. Glue the straw to the inside of the manger.

14 Using the template as a guide, glue the baby's body and head to the manger. Glue the halo to the head.

15 Make the round base. Roll forty 16-inch (40.6 cm) lengths of ¼-inch-wide (6 mm) beige quilling paper into a large tight circle; use the tuck and roll technique or glue the strips end to end to make it easier to roll. If you use the tuck and roll technique, after 20 strips, put a little glue on the end of the tucking strip so that the paper stays in place while rolling.

16 For the angel's stand, roll six 16-inch (40.6 cm) lengths of ¼-inch-wide (6 mm) beige quilling paper into a cone (Dome F) using the tuck and roll technique.

17 Glue the angel's stand, Mary, Joseph, and Baby Jesus to the base. Glue the angel to the stand.

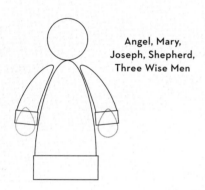

Angel, Mary, Joseph, Shepherd, Three Wise Men

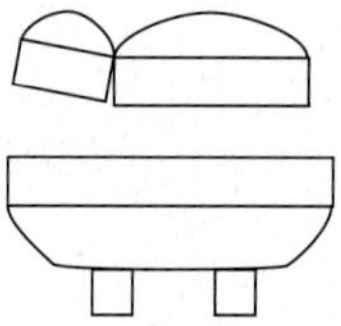

Baby Jesus and manger

1 For the Wise Man in green, make the following domes using the tuck and roll technique. Spread glue on the inside of the domes and let them dry.

- For the body, roll four 16-inch (40.6 cm) lengths of ¼-inch-wide (6 mm) forest-green quilling paper into a cone (Dome E). Wrap a strip of ⅛-inch-wide (3 mm) silver quilling paper around the bottom of the body.

- Make two arms. For each arm, roll one 16-inch (40.6 cm) length of ⅛-inch-wide (3 mm) forest-green quilling paper into a slightly curved cone. Wrap a strip of ⅛-inch-wide (3 mm) silver quilling paper around the cuff.

- Make two hands. For each hand, roll one 16-inch (40.6 cm) length of ⅛-inch-wide (3 mm) pale-peach quilling paper into a dome (Dome B). Pinch it into a teardrop.

- For the head, roll one 16-inch (40.6 cm) length of ⅛-inch-wide (3 mm) pale-peach quilling paper into a dome (Dome C).

- For the hair, roll one 16-inch (40.6 cm) length of ⅛-inch-wide (3 mm) light-brown quilling paper into a dome (Dome C).

2 For the hat, glue end-to-end an 8-inch (20.3 cm) length of ⅛-inch-wide (3 mm) metallic-silver quilling paper and an 8-inch (20.3 cm) length of ⅛-inch-wide (3 mm) forest-green quilling paper. Starting from the silver end, roll the paper into a dome (Dome B).

3 For the beard, trim a small triangle from the ¼-inch-wide (6 mm) light-brown quilling paper and glue it to the head.

4 Make the cup. For the bowl, roll a 16-inch (40.6 cm) length of ⅛-inch-wide (3 mm) gold quilling paper into a dome (Dome B). For the stem, roll a 1-inch (2.5 cm) length of ⅛-inch-wide (3 mm) gold quilling paper into a tight circle. For the base, roll a 12-inch (30.5 cm) length of ⅛-inch-wide (3 mm) gold quilling paper into a tight circle. Glue the bowl, stem, and base together.

- Make two arms. For each arm, roll one 16-inch (40.6 cm) length of ⅛-inch-wide (3 mm) royal-blue quilling paper into a slightly curved cone. Wrap a strip of ⅛-inch (3 mm) wide gold quilling paper around the cuff.

- Make two hands. For each hand, roll one 16-inch (40.6 cm) length of ⅛-inch-wide (3 mm) beige quilling paper into a dome (Dome B). Pinch it into a teardrop.

- For the head, roll one 16-inch (40.6 cm) length of ⅛-inch-wide (3 mm) beige quilling paper into a dome (Dome C).

- For the hair, roll one 16-inch (40.6 cm) length of ⅛-inch-wide (3 mm) brown quilling paper into a dome (Dome C).

7 For the crown, glue end-to-end a 4-inch (10.2 cm) length of ⅛-inch-wide (3 mm) gold quilling paper and a 16-inch (40.6 cm) length of ⅛-inch-wide (3 mm) royal-blue quilling paper. Starting from the royal-blue end, roll the paper into a dome (Dome B). For the outer edge of the crown, trim small triangular points in a 1-inch (2.5 cm) length of ⅛-inch-wide (3 mm) gold quilling paper and glue it to the crown.

8 For the beard, trim a small triangle from the ¼-inch-wide (6 mm) brown quilling paper. Glue it to the head.

9 Make the round treasure box. For the top, roll a 16-inch (40.6 cm) length of ⅛-inch-wide (3 mm) gold quilling paper into a dome (Dome B). For the bottom, roll a 12-inch (30.5 cm) length of ⅛-inch-wide (3 mm) gold quilling paper into a tight circle. For the handle, roll a 1-inch (2.5 cm) length of ⅛-inch-wide (3 mm) gold quilling paper into a tight circle. Glue the box top, bottom, and handle together.

5 Using the template as a guide, assemble the Wise Man in green. Glue the arms and hands to the body. Glue two halves of the head and hair together. Let them dry completely. Glue the head to the body, the hat to the head, and the cup to the hands.

6 For the Wise Man in royal blue, make the following domes using the tuck and roll technique. Spread glue on the inside of the domes and let them dry.

- For the body, roll four 16-inch (40.6 cm) lengths of ¼-inch-wide (6 mm) royal-blue quilling paper into a cone (Dome E). Wrap a strip of ⅛-inch-wide (3 mm) gold quilling paper around the bottom of the body.

Cup

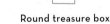

Round treasure box

Rectangular treasure box

10 Using the template as a guide, assemble the Wise Man in royal blue. Glue the arms and hands to the body. Glue two halves of the head and hair together. Let them dry completely. Then glue the head to the body, the crown to the head, and the round treasure box to the hands.

11 For the Wise Man in crimson, make the following domes using the tuck and roll technique. Spread glue on the inside of the domes and let them dry.

- For the body, roll four 16-inch (40.6 cm) lengths of ¼-inch-wide (6 mm) crimson quilling paper into a cone (Dome E). Wrap a strip of ⅛-inch-wide (3 mm) gold quilling paper around the bottom of the body.

- Make two arms. For each arm, roll one 16-inch (40.6 cm) length of ⅛-inch-wide (3 mm) crimson quilling paper into slightly curved cone. Wrap a strip of ⅛-inch-wide (3 mm) gold quilling paper around the cuff.

- Make two hands. For each hand, roll one 16-inch (40.6 cm) length of ⅛-inch-wide (3 mm) light-brown quilling paper into a dome (Dome B). Pinch it into a teardrop.

- For the head, roll one 16-inch (40.6 cm) length of ⅛-inch-wide (3 mm) light brown quilling paper into a dome (Dome C).

- For the hair, roll one 16-inch (40.6 cm) length of ⅛-inch-wide (3 mm) black quilling paper into a dome (Dome C).

12 For the crown, roll a 22-inch (45 cm) length of ⅛-inch-wide 3 mm) crimson quilling paper, using the end-to-end technique. For the crown of the hat, trim small triangular points in a ½-inch (1.3 cm) length of ¼-inch-wide (6 mm) platinum-white quilling paper and glue it to the crown. For the beard, trim a small triangle from the ¼-inch-wide (6 mm) brown quilling paper and glue it to the head. For the rectangular treasure box, roll a 16-inch (40.6 cm) length of ⅛-inch-wide (3 mm) silver quilling paper into a rectangle (CTB size 4); repeat. Stack and glue both rectangle pieces together. For the top, trim a small strip of ⅛-inch-wide (3 mm) silver quilling paper and glue it to the top of the box. For the box's handle, roll a 1-inch (2.5 cm) length of ⅛-inch-wide (3 mm) silver quilling paper into a tight circle. Glue the box and handle together.

13 Using the template as a guide, assemble the Wise Man in crimson. Glue the arms and hands to the body. Glue two halves of the head and hair together. Let them dry completely. Then glue the head to the body, the crown to the head, and the rectangular treasure box to the hands.

14 Make the round base. Roll fifty 16-inch (40.6 cm) lengths of ⅛-inch-wide (3 mm) sage-green quilling paper into a large tight circle; use the tuck and roll technique or glue the strips end-to-end to make it easier to roll. If you use the tuck and roll technique, after 20 strips, put a little glue on the end of the tucking strip so that the paper stays in place while rolling.

15 Glue the Wise Men onto the base.

Shepherd &Animals

1 For the sheep, make the following domes using the tuck and roll technique. Spread glue on the inside of the domes and let them dry.

- For the body, roll three 16-inch (40.6 cm) lengths of 1/8-inch-wide (3 mm) white quilling paper into a dome (Dome D).

- For the head, glue end-to-end a 1-inch (2.5 cm) length of 1/8-inch-wide (3 mm) black quilling paper to a 16-inch (40.6 cm) length of 1/8-inch-wide (3 mm) white quilling paper. Starting from the black end, roll it into a dome (Dome B).

- For each of the four feet, roll an 8-inch (20.3 cm) length of 1/8-inch-wide (3 mm) white quilling paper into a cone (Dome A). When the feet are dry, glue them together.

2 Make two ears. For each ear, roll a 2-inch (5.1 cm) length of 1/8-inch-wide (3 mm) white quilling paper into a teardrop. Glue the ears to the head.

3 Make the curly wool. Cut a 6-inch (15.2 cm) length of 1/8-inch-wide (3 mm) white quilling paper lengthwise to make two narrow strips. Trim the strips into 1-inch (2.5 cm) lengths and roll them into loose scrolls. Glue the scrolls to the body.

4 Using the template as a guide, glue the head to the body and the feet beneath the body.

5 For the donkey, make the following domes using the tuck and roll technique. Spread glue on the inside of the domes and let them dry.

- For the body, roll five 16-inch (40.6 cm) lengths of 1/8-inch-wide (3 mm) dark-gray quilling paper into a cone (Dome F) and roll five 16-inch (40.6 cm) lengths of 1/8-inch-wide (3 mm) dark gray quilling paper into a dome (Dome F). Glue the dome and cone together.

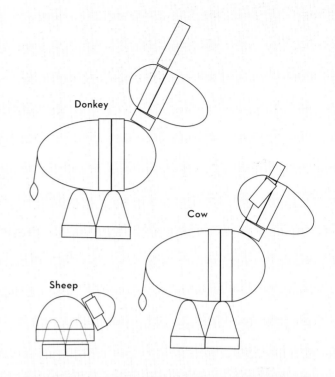

Donkey

Cow

Sheep

- For the front of the donkey's head, glue end-to-end a 16-inch (40.6 cm) length of 1/8-inch-wide (3 mm) gray and a 16-inch (40.6 cm) length of 1/8-inch-wide (3 mm) dark gray. Starting from the gray end, roll it into a cone (Dome C).

- For the back of the donkey's head, roll two (40.6 cm) lengths of 1/8-inch-wide (3 mm) dark-gray quilling paper into a dome (Dome C). When the halves are dry, glue them together.

- For each of the four feet, roll a 16-inch (40.6 cm) length of 1/8-inch-wide (3 mm) dark-gray quilling paper into a flattop cone (Dome B). Glue the feet together.

6 Make two ears. For each ear, roll a 6-inch (15.2 cm) length of 1/8-inch-wide (3 mm) gray quilling paper into a teardrop (CTB size 5). Glue the ears to the head.

7 For the neck, roll a 4-inch (10.2 cm) length of 1/8-inch-wide (3 mm) dark-gray quilling paper into a loose circle (CTB size 6). Glue the neck between the head and body.

8 For the tail, roll a 3-inch (7.6 cm) length of 1/8-inch-wide (3 mm) dark-gray quilling paper into a loose scroll, leaving 1/2 inch (1.3 cm) from the end section straight. Pinch the scroll into a marquise, and glue the marquise to the straight section.

9 Using the template as a guide, glue the tail, body, and feet together.

10 For the cow, make the following domes using the tuck and roll technique. Spread glue on the inside of the domes and let them dry.

- For the body, roll five 16-inch (40.6 cm) lengths of 1/8-inch-wide (3 mm) ivory quilling paper into a cone (Dome F). Repeat to make another ivory cone for the other half of the body. Glue the cones together.

- For the front of the cow's head, glue end-to-end a 16-inch (40.6 cm) length of 1/8-inch-wide (3 mm) gray quilling paper and a 16-inch (40.6 cm) length of 1/8-inch-wide (3 mm) pale-pink quilling paper. Starting from the pale-pink end, roll it into a cone (Dome C). For the back of the cow's head, roll two 16-inch (40.6 cm) lengths of ivory quilling paper into a dome (Dome C). When both pieces are dry, glue them together.

- For each of the four feet, glue end-to-end a 2-inch (5.1 cm) length of 1/8-inch-wide (3 mm) black quilling paper and a 16-inch (40.6 cm) length of 1/8-inch-wide (3 mm) ivory quilling paper. Starting from the ivory end, roll it into a flattop cone (Dome B). Glue the feet together.

11 Make two ears. For each ear, roll a 4-inch (10.2 cm) length of 1/8-inch-wide (3 mm) black quilling paper into a half circle (CTB size 6). Glue the ears to the head.

12 For the neck, roll a 4-inch (10.2 cm) length of 1/8-inch-wide (3 mm) ivory quilling paper into a loose circle (CTB size 6). Glue the neck between the head and body.

13 For the tail, roll a 3-inch (7.6 cm) length of 1/8-inch-wide (3 mm) black quilling paper into a loose scroll, leaving 1/2 inch (1.3 cm) from the end straight. Pinch the scroll into a marquise and glue the marquise to the straight section.

14 For the spots, cut two 16-inch (40.6 cm) lengths of 1/8-inch-wide (3 mm) black quilling paper lengthwise to make narrow strips. Trim the narrow strips into 8-inch (20.3 cm) lengths and 4-inch (10.2 cm) lengths to make different-size spots on the cow. Roll them into loose circles and pinch them into random shapes. Glue them to the body.

15 Using the template as a guide, glue the tail, body, and feet together.

16 For the shepherd, make the following domes using the tuck and roll technique. Spread glue on the inside of the domes and let them dry.

- For the body, roll four 16-inch (40.6 cm) lengths of 1/4-inch-wide (6 mm) light-brown quilling paper into a cone (Dome E).

- Make two arms. For each arm, roll one 16-inch (40.6 cm) length of 1/4-inch-wide (6 mm) brown quilling paper into a slightly curved cone (Dome B).

- Make two hands. For each hand, roll one 16-inch (40.6 cm) length of 1/8-inch-wide (3 mm) pale-peach quilling paper into a dome (Dome B). Pinch it into a teardrop.

- For the head, roll one 16-inch (40.6 cm) length of 1/8-inch-wide (3 mm) pale-peach quilling paper into a dome (Dome C).

- For the hair, roll one 16-inch (40.6 cm) length of light-brown quilling paper into a dome (Dome C).

17 For the staff, use the banding technique to wrap an 8-inch (20.3 cm) length of beige quilling paper around a 3-inch (7.6 cm) length of beige quilling paper. Trim to 2 inches (5.1 cm) and curl the end.

18 For the headscarf, cut a 1½-inch (3.8 cm) length of ¼-inch-wide (6 mm) brown quilling paper.

19 Using the template as a guide, assemble the Shepherd. Glue the arms and hands to the body. Glue two halves of the head and hair together. Let them dry completely. Then glue the head to the body, the headscarf to the head, and the staff to the hand.

20 Make the round base. Roll fifty 16-inch (40.6 cm) lengths of ⅛-inch-wide (3 mm) brown quilling paper into a large tight circle; use the tuck and roll technique or glue the strips end-to-end to make it easier to roll. If you use the tuck and roll technique, after 20 strips, put a little glue on the end of the tucking strip so that the paper stays in place while rolling.

21 Glue the shepherd and animals to the base.

Nutcracker
FIGURINE

This beloved Nutcracker has always been a symbol of good luck and protection. Discover the fun and challenge of creating the typically wooden toy soldier using large tight circles of paper strips!

hard

6¾" TALL
(17.1 cm)

What You Need

Basic Quilling Tool Kit (page 10)

Quilling paper, ¼ inch (6 mm) wide: black, white, red, metallic gold, pale peach

Mini Mold

Quilling paper, ⅛ inch (3 mm) wide: red, metallic gold, pale peach, black, white, deep blue

Template

Ink pad: gold

Chalk: red

Cotton swab

Quilling Shapes

tight circle   *teardrop*   *marquise*   *half circle*

curved teardrop   *triangle*   *tight oval*

Techniques

Large Tight Circle: Tuck and Roll (page 19)

Flattop Cone (page 21)

Dish (page 21)

Cutting Narrow Strips (page 24)

Dome (page 20)

Attaching End-to-End (page 15)

What You Do

1   To make the shaft of each boot, roll three large tight circles using two 16-inch (40.6 cm) lengths of ¼-inch-wide (6 mm) black quilling paper for each circle. Stack the three circles with the seams aligned.

2   To make each foot, roll a large tight circle (CTB size 1) using three 16-inch (40.6 cm) lengths of ¼-inch-wide (6 mm) black quilling paper (CTB size 1). Pinch each large circle into a teardrop.

3   To make each leg, roll seven large tight circles using two 16-inch (40.6 cm) lengths of ¼-inch-wide (6 mm) white quilling paper for each circle. Stack the circles with the seams aligned.

4   With the boot and leg seams facing the back, glue the shafts, feet, and legs together.

5   Make the Nutcracker's body. For the hips, roll twelve 16-inch (40.6 cm) lengths of ¼-inch-wide (6 mm) red quilling paper into a flattop cone (Dome J). For the lower chest, roll fifteen 16-inch (40.6 cm) lengths of ¼-inch-wide (6 mm) red quilling paper into a flattop cone. The flat portion of the lower chest should be the same size as the flat portion of the hip. Spread glue on the inside of each cone and let it dry. For the upper chest, roll fifteen 16-inch (40.6 cm) lengths of ⅛-inch-wide (3 mm) red quilling paper into a dish. Spread glue on the inside of the dish and let it dry. Glue the hips, lower chest, and upper chest together, as shown in the template.

6   Make the belt. For the strap, wrap a 6-inch (7.6 cm) length of ¼-inch-wide (6 mm) black quilling paper around the waist twice. For the left and right sides of the buckle, trim two ¼-inch (6 mm) lengths of ⅛-inch-wide (3 mm) gold quilling paper. Glue the lengths onto the strap. For the top and bottom sides of the buckle, cut a ⅜-inch (9 mm) length of ⅛-inch-wide (3 mm) gold quilling paper in half lengthwise to make two narrow strips. Glue the narrow strips to the strap.

7   Glue the body with the belt to the legs.

Circle Templates

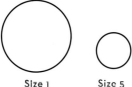

Size 1   Size 5

8 For each shoulder, arm, and cuff, you will use ¼-inch-wide (6 mm) quilling paper. To make each shoulder, roll a 16-inch (40.6 cm) length of ¼-inch-wide (6 mm) gold quilling paper into a large tight circle. To make each arm, roll four tight circles using two 16-inch (40.6 cm) lengths of ¼-inch-wide (6 mm) red quilling paper for each tight circle. Glue the circles on top of each other with the seams aligned. For each cuff, roll a tight circle using two 16-inch (40.6 cm) lengths of ¼-inch-wide (6 mm) black quilling paper. Glue the shoulder and cuff to the arm.

9 Glue the completed shoulders and arms to the side of the body.

10 To make each hand, roll two 16-inch (40.6 cm) lengths of ⅛-inch-wide (3 mm) pale-peach quilling paper into a dome (Dome C). Spread glue on the inside of each dome and let it dry. Glue it to the cuff with the inside of the dome facing front.

11 Make the head. For the top half of the head, roll twelve 16-inch (40.6 cm) lengths of ¼-inch-wide (6 mm) pale peach quilling paper into a flattop cone. For the bottom half, roll twelve 16-inch (40.6 cm) lengths of ⅛-inch-wide (3 mm) pale-peach quilling paper into a dish. Spread glue on the inside of the flattop cone and dish and let them dry. Glue the two halves together and let dry. Glue the head to the body.

12 Make the hat. For the rim of the hat, roll ten 16-inch (40.6 cm) lengths of ⅛-inch-wide (3 mm) gold quilling paper into a tight circle. For the bottom, roll ten 16-inch (40.6 cm) lengths of ¼-inch-wide (6 mm) black quilling paper into a flattop cone. For the top, roll ten 16-inch (40.6 cm) lengths of ⅛-inch-wide (3 mm) black quilling paper into a dish. Spread glue on the inside of the flattop cone and dish and let them dry. Glue the black

halves of the hat together, and then glue the gold rim to the bottom of the hat. When the hat is dry, glue it to the head.

13 For the hair, cut thirty 1½-inch (3.8 cm) lengths of ¼-inch-wide (6 mm) white quilling paper. Cut them into the shape shown in the template and slightly curl each length. Glue them around the head.

14 For the Nutcracker's beard, you will use two 1½-inch (3.8 cm) lengths of ¼-inch-wide (6 mm) white quilling paper. Cut fringe onto one end of the lengths. Glue each length side by side to the Nutcracker's chin. With scissors, cut the bottom of the beard fringe into a V shape.

15 For the mouth, glue a ½-inch (1.3 cm) length of ¼-inch-wide (6 mm) red quilling paper to the top of the beard.

16 For the teeth, cut an 8-inch (20.3 cm) length of ⅛-inch-wide (3 mm) white quilling paper lengthwise to make two narrow strips. Cut the narrow strips into eight 1½-inch (3.8 cm) lengths. Roll each length into tight ovals. Glue them to the mouth in two rows, each with four tight ovals.

17 For the mustache, cut a 6-inch (15.2 cm) length of ⅛-inch-wide (3 mm) black quilling paper lengthwise to make two narrow strips. Roll each strip into a curved teardrop (CTB size 5). Glue the mustache above the teeth.

18 For the nose, roll a 6-inch (15.2 cm) length of ⅛-inch-wide (3 mm) pale-peach quilling paper into a narrow triangle (CTB size 5). Glue the nose to the center of the head.

19 To make each eyebrow, cut a 3-inch (7.6 cm) length of ⅛-inch-wide (3 mm) black quilling paper lengthwise to make two narrow strips. Roll each strip into a teardrop.

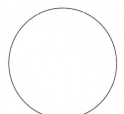

Approximate size of the tight circle for the upper and lower chest

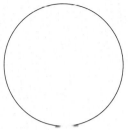

Approximate size of the tight circle for the hat, rim, and face

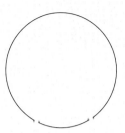

Approximate size of the tight circle for the hips

Approximate size of the tight circle for the shoulder, arms, cuffs, and hands

Approximate size of the tight circle for the legs and boots

Foot

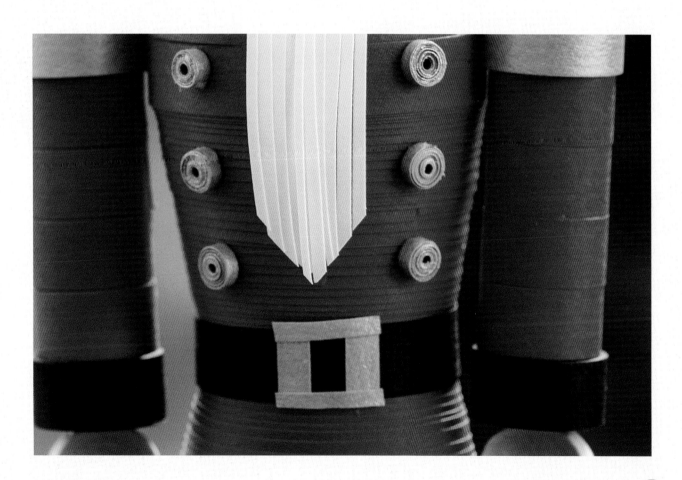

Glue each eyebrow beneath the rim of the hat.

20 To make the eyes, glue end-to-end a 1-inch (2.5 cm) length of ¹⁄₈-inch-wide (3 mm) black quilling paper, a 2-inch (5.1 cm) length of ¹⁄₈-inch-wide (3 mm) deep blue, and a 4-inch (10.2 cm) length of ¹⁄₈-inch-wide (3 mm) white quilling paper together. Trim the entire length in half lengthwise to make two narrow strips, one for each eye. Starting from the black end, roll the paper into a half circle. Glue each eye beneath the eyebrows.

21 Make six gold buttons. For each button, cut a 6-inch (15.2 cm) length of ¹⁄₈-inch-wide (3 mm) gold quilling paper lengthwise to make two narrow strips. Cut each narrow strip into six 3-inch (7.6 cm) lengths. Roll the lengths into tight circles. Add gold ink to the edges of the buttons. Glue three buttons on each side of the Nutcracker's chest.

22 For the hat's insignia, cut a 6-inch (15.2 cm) length of ¹⁄₈-inch-wide (3 mm) gold quilling paper lengthwise to make two narrow strips. Cut five 3-inch (7.6 cm) lengths. Roll the lengths into marquises. Glue them together and add gold ink to the edges. For the red gem, cut a 3-inch (7.6 cm) length of ¹⁄₈-inch-wide (3 mm) red quilling paper lengthwise to make a narrow strip and roll it into a tight circle. Glue the red gem to the gold insignia. Glue the insignia to the center of the hat.

23 For the Nutcracker's rosy cheeks, dab some red chalk above his mustache with the cotton swab.

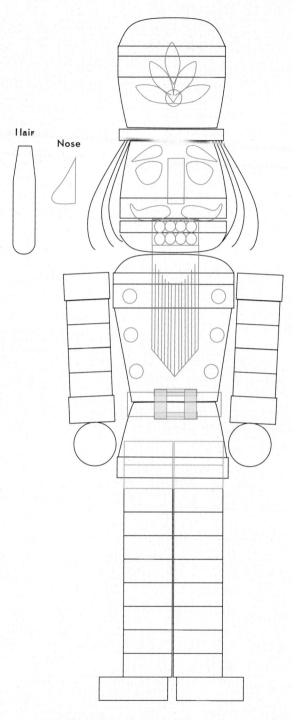

Hair

Nose

Note: Paper thicknesses vary slightly, depending on the color of the paper. Therefore, the final size of a large tight circle may be slightly different, even if the paper lengths are the same. The size differences will not affect the final design.

Ornaments & Stocking Stuffers

Heart & Teardrop
SNOWFLAKE ORNAMENTS

Add these dainty snowflakes to your ornament collection. The swirling circles and shiny rhinestones will brighten up any Christmas tree.

easy

2" × 2"
(5.1 × 5.1 cm)

What You Need

Basic Quilling Tool Kit (page 10)

Template

Quilling paper, 1/8 inch (3 mm) wide: white

14 rhinestones

2 jump rings

Pliers

Cording: silver

Quilling Shapes

arrow   *heart*   *tight circle*

diamond   *teardrop*

Techniques

Gluing Back Sides
for a Freestanding Piece (page 21)

Off-Center Circles (page 17)

Circle Templates

Size 3   Size 6

Snowflake with Hearts

1   Lay out the template between the corkboard and a sheet of wax paper.

2   Make six arms for the center of the snowflake. For the bottom half of each arm, roll an 8-inch (20.3 cm) length of white quilling paper into a long arrow (CTB size 3). Glue the points of the arrows together.

3   For the next layer, roll six small arrows (CTB size 6) using a 4-inch (10.2 cm) length of white quilling paper for each. Glue the small arrows with their points facing outward between the long arrows.

4   Make six large hearts. For each large heart, roll an 8-inch (20.3 cm) length of white quilling paper into a heart shape (CTB size 3). Glue them to the long arrows with the point of each heart facing outward.

5   Roll seven tight circles. Use a 2-inch (5.1 cm) length of white quilling paper for each tight circle. Glue six of them on the points of the small arrows and one to the middle of the snowflake.

6   Spread glue over the heart and arrow-shaped pieces to prevent the coils from falling out. Let it dry.

7   Glue small rhinestones to the tight circles.

8   Use pliers to hold and bend a jump ring open. Insert the jump ring into one of the heart pieces and bend it closed. Tie the silver cording around the jump ring to hang the ornament.

Snowflake with Hearts

Snowflake with Teardrops

1   Lay out the template between the corkboard and a sheet of wax paper.

2   Make the center of the snowflake. Roll six diamonds (CTB size 3) using an 8-inch (20.3 cm) length of white quilling paper for each. Glue the points of the diamonds together.

3   Make six off-center teardrops. For each off-center teardrop, start by rolling an 8-inch (20.3 cm) length of white quilling paper into an off-center circle (CTB size 3). Then pinch each off-center circle into a teardrop shape. Glue each off-center teardrop between the points of two diamonds.

4   Make six teardrops for the outer points. For each one, roll an 8-inch (20.3 cm) length of white quilling paper into a loose or tight coil (CTB size 6) and pinch it into a teardrop.

5   Roll a 2-inch (5.1 cm) length of white quilling paper into a tight circle and glue it to the center of the snowflake.

Snowflake with Teardrops

6   Glue small rhinestones to the small teardrop points of the snowflake.

7   Use pliers to hold and bend a jump ring open. Insert the jump ring into one of the teardrop pieces and bend it closed. Tie the silver cording around the jump ring to hang the ornament.

Round Poinsettia
ORNAMENT

This project shows that a cookie cutter is perfect for
making borders. Fill this round border with quilled
shapes to make an eye-catching ornament.

medium

2" × 2¼"
(5.1 × 5.7 cm)

What You Need

Basic Quilling Tool Kit (page 10)

Template

Quilling paper, ⅛ inch (3 mm) wide:
sage green, red, yellow

Round cookie cutter,
2 inches (5.1 cm) in diameter

Jump ring

Pliers

Cording: gold

Quilling Shapes

tight circle

marquise

rectangle

*double
scroll*

Techniques

Border (page 17)

Gluing Back Sides
for a Freestanding Piece (page 21)

Circle Templates

Size 2

Size 6

What You Do

1 Lay the template between the corkboard and a sheet of wax paper.

2 Make the outline of the ornament. Wrap a 16-inch (40.6 cm) length of sage-green quilling paper around the cookie cutter twice. Glue the ends together. When the glue is dry, remove the paper from the cookie cutter.

3 Make three small poinsettias. For each small poinsettia, roll three 4-inch (10.2 cm) lengths of red quilling paper into marquises (CTB size 6). Glue the marquises together at one end. For the center of each flower, roll three tight circles using a 2-inch (5.1 cm) length of yellow quilling paper for each. Glue the tight circles to the three petals.

4 Make three large poinsettias. For each large poinsettia, roll six 4-inch (10.2 cm) lengths of red quilling paper into marquises (CTB size 6). Glue the marquises together at one end. For the center of each flower, roll four tight circles using a 2-inch (5.1 cm) length of yellow quilling paper for each. Glue the tight circles to the six petals.

5 Make nine double scrolls. Use a 2-inch (5.1 cm) length of sage-green quilling paper for each scroll.

6 Arrange all the pieces inside the round border, as shown in the template. Apply glue to the spots where the pieces touch each other.

7 For the ornament's top, roll a 12-inch (30.5 cm) length of sage-green quilling paper into a rectangle (CTB size 2). Glue it to the ornament and spread additional glue over the coils so that they do not fall out. Let it dry.

8 Use pliers to hold and bend a jump ring open. Insert the jump ring into one of the teardrop pieces and bend it closed. Tie the gold cording around the jump ring to hang the ornament.

Holiday Light Bulb
ORNAMENTS

The beehive technique and two-tone quilling papers create these colorful ornaments. The black border also gives them a stained-glass effect.

What You Need

Basic Quilling Tool Kit (page 10)

Template

Quillography paper, ⅛ inch (3 mm)
wide: black

Quilling paper, ⅛ inch (3 mm) wide:
Highlights by Quilled Creations in
blue/purple, pink/purple, yellow/
blue, and orange/red

Round cookie cutter,
2 inches (5.1 cm) in diameter

2 jump rings

Pliers

Cording: multicolored metallic

Quilling Shapes

teardrop   *marquise*   *rectangle*

Techniques

Border (page 17)

Beehive Swirls (page 18)

Gluing Back Sides
for a Freestanding Piece (page 21)

Circle Templates

Size 2   Size 3

What You Do

1 Lay the template between the corkboard and a sheet of wax paper.

2 Make the outline of the ornament. Wrap a 16-inch (40.6 cm) length of black quillography strip around the cookie cutter twice. Glue the ends together. Once the glue is dry, remove the circle from the cookie cutter and shape it into a teardrop.

3 Make the middle section of the ornament. Roll six 8-inch (20.3 cm) lengths of blue/purple quilling paper with the blue on the outside into marquises (CTB size 3). Glue them inside the center section of the template.

4 Make a black border above and below the marquises using the black quillography strip. Cut two strips, about 2 inches (5.1 cm) in length so that they divide the teardrop-shaped border into three sections. Glue the ends to the border at the sides of the teardrop-shaped outline.

5 Roll four 16-inch (40.6 cm) lengths of pink/purple quilling paper with the purple on the outside with the beehive technique. Fill the top and bottom spaces with the beehive curls.

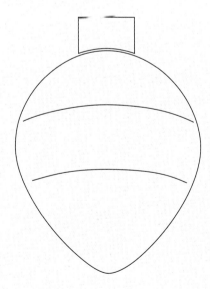

6 For the ornament's hanger, roll a 16-inch (40.6 cm) length of blue/purple quilling paper into a rectangle with the blue on the outside (CTB size 2). Glue it to the top of the ornament and spread additional glue over the coils so that they do not fall out.

7 Spread a light layer of glue over the entire ornament. Let it dry.

8 Use pliers to hold and bend a jump ring open. Insert the jump ring into one of the teardrop pieces and bend it closed. Tie the cording around the jump ring to hang the ornament.

9 To make the orange ornament, repeat steps 1–7 using the yellow/blue quilling paper for the middle marquise and the top sections and orange/red paper with the orange on the outside for the top and bottom sections.

Poinsettia
PIN

No flower says Christmas like the stunning poinsettia.
Get ready for all of the compliments when you wear this
quilled beauty at holiday parties!

What You Need

Basic Quilling Tool Kit (page 10)

Template

Quilling paper, ⅛ inch (3 mm) wide:
sage green, red, deep yellow

Mini Mold

Pin backing

Quilling Shapes

marquise   *flat half
circle*   *tight circle*

Techniques

Dome (page 20)

Gluing Back Sides
for a Freestanding Piece (page 21)

Circle Templates

Size 1   Size 3

What You Do

1 Lay the template between the corkboard and a sheet of wax paper.

2 Make the flower's center. Roll six 8-inch (20.3 cm) lengths of sage-green quilling paper into marquises (CTB size 3). Glue the six marquises together at the points on one end.

3 Make 12 petals. For each petal, roll two 16-inch (40.6 cm) lengths of red quilling paper into flat half circles (CTB size 1). Glue the edges of two flat half circles together and let them dry.

4 Glue six petals around the flower's center as shown in the template. Glue the second layer of petals on top. The petals in the second layer should rest between the petals on the first layer.

5 Make seven stamens. For each stamen, roll a 4-inch (10.2 cm) length of deep yellow quilling paper into a tight circle. Shape it into a dome (Dome A). Gently spread glue inside the dome and let it dry. Once dry, glue it to the center of the flower, domed side up.

6 Spread glue on the back of the flower and let it dry completely.

7 Glue the pin backing to the back of the flower.

Petal

Pieces in gray are on
top of the base layer.

Tip

Create this flower in other Christmas colors! Make a bouquet of poinsettias with ivory and crimson quilling paper. Thread a string through a petal from each poinsettia, and this beautiful flower chain can be hung on a Christmas tree.

Snowman
ORNAMENT

This cool snowman is ready to hang out on your tree or on top of a gift box. Create adorable winter accessories for the snowman with the crimping and banding techniques.

What You Need

Basic Quilling Tool Kit (page 10)

Template

Quilling paper, ¼ inch (6 mm) wide:
white, royal blue, teal

Mini Mold

Quilling paper, ⅛ inch (3 mm) wide:
orange, black, teal

Template

Cording: silver

Quilling Shape

tight circle

Techniques

Large Tight Circle: Tuck and Roll
(page 19)

Dome (page 20)

Cutting Narrow Strips (page 24)

Banding (page 23)

Crimping (page 18)

What You Do

1 Make the snowman's body. Using the tuck and roll technique, roll fifteen 16-inch (40.6 cm) lengths of white quilling paper into a tight circle. Shape it into a dome (Dome K). Spread glue on the inside and let it dry. Repeat to make the other half of the body. Glue the two domes together.

2 Make the head. Using the tuck and roll technique, roll eight 16-inch (40.6 cm) lengths of white quilling paper into a tight circle. Shape it into a dome (Dome I). Spread glue on the inside and let it dry. Repeat to make the other half of the head. Glue the two domes together, then glue the head and body together.

3 Make the snowman's nose. Roll an 8-inch (20.3 cm) length of orange quilling paper into a tight circle. Use tweezers to help shape it into a long cone, using the template as a guide. Glue the nose to the head.

4 Make the snowman's eyes and mouth. Cut an 8-inch (20.3 cm) length of black quilling paper lengthwise to make two narrow strips, then trim the narrow strips into two 4-inch (10.2 cm) and four 2-inch (5.1 cm) lengths. For each eye, roll a 4-inch (10.2 cm) length of narrow black quilling paper into a tight circle. For the mouth, roll four 2-inch (5.1 cm) lengths of narrow black quilling paper into tight circles. With the template as reference, glue the eyes and mouth to the head.

5 Make the scarf. Use the banding technique to wrap a 16-inch (40.6 cm) length of ⅛-inch-wide (3 mm) teal quilling paper around a 16-inch (40.6 cm) length of ¼-inch-wide (6 mm) royal-blue quilling paper. Trim the scarf to 10 inches (25.4 cm). Wrap the scarf around the snowman's neck and glue it in place.

6 Make the hat. Crimp the following 16-inch (40.6 cm) lengths of ¼-inch (6 mm) strips with a crimper (large crimp size): two royal blue, two teal, and one white. Gently roll the crimped strips into tight circles. Hold the edge of the paper to avoid flattening the strip. Roll the strips, alternating the strips in this pattern: royal blue, teal, white, royal blue, and teal. Knot and loop a 6-inch (15.2 cm) piece of silver cording. Carefully insert the silver cording into the center of the hat with the knot on the inside of the hat. Shape the coil into a dome (Dome H). Spread glue on the inside of the dome and on the knot and then place it on the snowman's head.

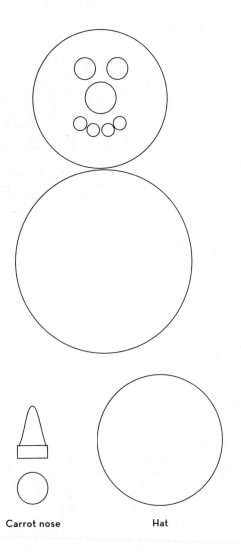

Carrot nose   Hat

Silver Bell
ORNAMENT

Hang this classic symbol or give it as a gift to spread
Christmas cheer everywhere.

What You Need

Basic Quilling Tool Kit (page 10)

Quilling paper, ¼ inch (6 mm) wide:
metallic silver

Quilling paper, ⅛ inch (3 mm) wide:
metallic silver, sage green, crimson

Template

Mini Mold

Cording: silver

Quilling Shapes

holly leaf   *tight circle*

Techniques

Large Tight Circle: Tuck and Roll
(page 19)

Dome (page 20)

Circle Template

Size 1

What You Do

1 For the bell, roll twenty 16-inch (40.6 cm) lengths of ¼-inch-wide (6 mm) silver quilling paper into a large tight circle using the tuck and roll technique. Shape the circle into a bell shape using the template as a guide. Spread glue on the inside of the bell and let it dry.

2 For the clapper, make two domes. For each dome, roll a 16-inch (40.6 cm) length of ⅛-inch-wide (3 mm) silver quilling paper into a tight circle. Shape each coil into a dome (Dome B). Spread glue on the inside of each dome and let it dry.

3 Cut a 6-inch (15.2 cm) length of silver cording and fold it in half to make a loop. Insert the ends of the loop through the top of the bell. Tie the ends hanging inside the bell into a large knot.

4 To hang the clapper inside the bell, glue the bottoms of the two domes around the knot, as shown in the template, and let dry.

5 Make three holly leaves and three berries. For each holly leaf, roll a 16-inch (40.6 cm) length of sage-green quilling paper into a holly leaf (CTB size 1). For each berry, roll an 8-inch (20.3 cm) length of crimson quilling paper into a tight circle. Shape the tight circle into a dome (Dome A). Spread glue on the inside of the dome and let it dry. Glue the holly leaves and berries around the top of the bell.

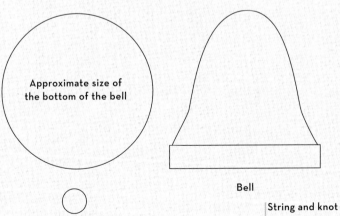

Approximate size of
the bottom of the bell

Bell

String and knot

Berry and holly

Clapper

Diamond-Center Snowflake
ORNAMENT

Here's another gorgeous snowflake to hang on the tree
or from a window. Its multilayered scrolls and nesting
diamond borders create a very stylish design.

hard

4" × 4"
(10.2 × 10.2 cm)

What You Need

Basic Quilling Tool Kit (page 10)

Quilling paper, ⅛ inch (3 mm) wide:
white

Template

Border Buddy

Jump ring

Pliers

Cording: silver

Quilling Shapes

arrow

tight circle

star

Techniques

Border (page 17)

Multilayered Scroll (page 22)

Gluing Back Sides
for a Freestanding Piece (page 23)

Circle Template

Size 3

What You Do

1 Lay the template between the corkboard and a sheet of wax paper.

2 Make six concentric three-piece diamonds for the center of the snowflake. For each small diamond border, wrap a 4-inch (10.2 cm) length of white quilling paper around the Border Buddy (size 10). For each medium diamond border, wrap a 6-inch (15.2 cm) length of white quilling paper around the Border Buddy (size 8). For each large diamond border, wrap an 8-inch (20.3 cm) length of white quilling paper around the Border Buddy (size 6). Glue a small and medium diamond border inside each large diamond border at a pointed end. Glue the concentric diamonds together with their glued points facing the center, using the template as a guide.

3 Roll six 8-inch (20.3 cm) lengths of white quilling paper into arrows (CTB size 3). Glue the arrows between the concentric diamonds with their points facing the center, using the template as a guide.

4 Roll six 4-inch (10.2 cm) lengths of white quilling paper into tight circles. Glue the tight circles to the arrows, using the template as a guide.

5 Make 12 multilayered scrolls. For each scroll, glue three 2-inch (5.1 cm) lengths of white quilling paper together at one end. Use the multilayered scroll technique to roll the strips. Glue the end of each scroll to the point of each arrow piece.

6 Make six snowflake points. For each snowflake point, roll an 8-inch (20.3 cm) length of white quilling paper into a star (CTB size 3). Glue the diamonds between the scrolls, using the template as a guide.

7   Roll an 8-inch (20.3 cm) length of white quilling paper into a tight circle. Glue it to the center of the snowflake.

8   Spread glue on the back of the snowflake points and arrow piece. Let it dry.

9   Use pliers to hold and bend a jump ring open. Insert the jump ring into one of the teardrop pieces and bend it closed. Tie the silver cording around the jump ring to hang the ornament.

Christmas Lights
JEWELRY SET

Crazy holiday sweaters are all the rage at holiday parties. So, why not complement one with some festive Christmas jewelry. These also make cute gift toppers!

hard

NECKLACE: 16" LONG
(40.6 cm)
EARRINGS: 2" LONG
(5.1 cm)

What You Need

Basic Quilling Tool Kit (page 10)

Quilling paper, ⅛ inch (3 mm) wide:
red, blush, forest green, orange,
melon, deep yellow, pale yellow, leaf
green, mint green, deep blue, light
blue, purple, lilac

Template

Round cookie cutter,
1½ inches (3.8 cm) in diameter

6 jump rings

Necklace cording,
16 inches (40.6 cm) long

Pliers

2 hanging earring findings

Quilling Shape

rectangle

Techniques

Border (page 17)

Looping (page 16)

Gluing Back Sides
for a Freestanding Piece (page 23)

Circle Template

Size 3

What You Do

1   Lay the template between the corkboard and a sheet of
    wax paper.

2   Make the outline of the red Christmas light. Wrap a 16-inch
    (40.6 cm) length of red quilling paper around the cookie
    cutter. Glue the ends together. Once the glue is dry, remove
    the circle from the cookie cutter and pinch it into a teardrop
    shape.

3   Make five eight-looped pieces. For each piece, hand-loop
    a 16-inch (40.6 cm) length of red quilling paper, using the
    template to determine the final length of the loop. Pinch
    each piece to flatten and place the flattened loops in the
    bottom half of the Christmas light. Glue the bottoms of the
    loops to the tip of the teardrop-shaped border.

4   Make five six-looped pieces for the top half of the light bulb.
    For each piece, hand-loop an 8-inch (20.3 cm) length of red
    quilling paper. Place the pieces inside the border, alternating
    each six-looped piece with an eight-looped piece.

5   Make the "glare." Use an 8-inch (20.3 cm) length of blush
    quilling paper and hand-loop the entire strip to make a six-
    looped piece. Place the glare in the position shown in the
    template.

6   Make the bulb's socket. Roll an 8-inch (20.3 cm) length of
    forest-green quilling paper into a rectangle (CTB size 3).
    Glue it to the top of the light bulb.

7   Spread glue on the edges of the entire ornament and along
    the border to hold the pieces in place. Let it dry.

8   Repeat steps 2–7 to make Christmas lights with the other
    quilling paper colors in the following combinations:

BULB COLOR	GLARE COLOR
Orange	Melon
Deep yellow	Pale yellow
Leaf green	Mint green
Deep blue	Light blue
Purple	Lilac

9 Use pliers to hold and bend the jump rings open. Insert a jump ring into each Christmas light and bend them closed.

10 Assemble the necklace. String four lights through the necklace cording with the "glare" of each light facing the same direction. Tighten the jump ring around the cord with pliers. Make sure the bulbs are evenly spaced.

For each earring, attach the jump ring to a hanging earring finding.

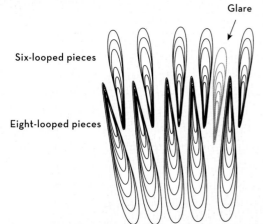

Glare

Six-looped pieces

Eight-looped pieces

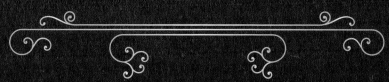

Greeting Cards & Gift Packaging

REASON FOR THE SEAS

Christmas Tree
CARD

Holidays are extra special when you send a handmade greeting card to your friends or loved ones. Create a fancy Christmas tree with quilled coils that will bring a smile to their faces!

easy

7" × 5"
(17.8 × 12.7 cm)

What You Need

Basic Quilling Tool Kit (page 10)

Card stock: white

Ink pad: green

Quilling paper, ⅛ inch (3 mm) wide:
yellow, crimson, sage green, light
brown

Template

Quilling Shapes

diamond   *loose circle*   *triangle*

Techniques

Multilayered Scroll (page 22)

Attaching End-to-End (page 15)

Circle Templates

Size 1   Size 6

What You Do

1   Cut out a 7 × 10-inch (17.8 × 25.4 cm) rectangle from the white card stock. Score the middle of the card vertically and fold it in half. Ink the edges with the green ink.

2   Make the tree's star. Roll five 4-inch (10.2 cm) lengths of yellow quilling paper into diamonds (CTB size 6). Glue them together.

3   Make six red berries. For each berry, roll a 4-inch (5 cm) length of crimson quilling paper into a loose circle (CTB size 6).

4   Make the first layer of branches. For each branch, glue three 2-inch (5.1 cm) lengths of sage-green quilling paper. Use the multilayered scroll technique to roll the strips.

5   Make the second layer of branches. For each branch, glue three 3-inch (7.6 cm) lengths of sage-green quilling paper together. Use the multilayered scroll technique to roll the strips.

6   Make the third layer of branches. For each branch, glue three 4-inch (10.2 cm) lengths of sage-green quilling paper together end-to-end. Use the multilayered scroll technique to roll the strips.

7   Make the fourth layer of branches. For each branch, glue three 5-inch (12.5 cm) lengths of sage-green quilling paper together. Use the multilayered scroll technique to roll the strips.

8   Make the fifth layer of branches. For each branch, glue three 6-inch (15.2 cm) lengths of sage-green quilling paper together. Use the multilayered scroll technique to roll the strips.

9   For the trunk, roll a 16-inch (40.6 cm) length of light-brown quilling paper into a triangle (CTB size 1).

10 Using the template as a reference, glue the star, branches, berries, and trunk on the front of the card.

Layer 1

Layer 2

Layer 3

Layer 4

Layer 5

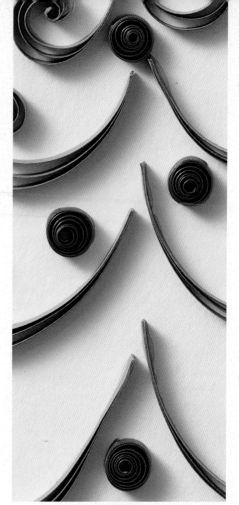

Christmas Wreath
CARD

With only two quilled shapes, you can make a card that will amaze your gift recipient. Plus, they won't believe the wreath is actually made with simple strips of paper.

believe

What You Need

Basic Quilling Tool Kit (page 10)

Card stock: red, light brown

Ink pad: green

Quilling paper, ⅛ inch (3 mm) wide:
leaf green, red

Template

Pencil

Round cookie cutter,
2½ inches (6.4 cm) in diameter

Felt-tip pen: black

Quilling Shapes

*curved
marquise*   *tight circle*

Circle Template

Size 3

What You Do

1 Cut out a 4½ × 9-inch (11.4 × 22.9 cm) rectangle from the red card stock. Score the middle of the card vertically and fold it in half.

2 Cut out a 4 × 4-inch (10.2 × 10.2 cm) rectangle from the light-brown card stock and round the edges with scissors. Ink the edges of the light-brown rectangle with green ink. Center the light-brown rectangle on the front of the red card, and glue the two pieces together.

3 Make 35 leaves. For each leaf, roll an 8-inch (20.3 cm) length of leaf-green quilling paper into curved marquises (CTB size 3). Glue the points of three leaves together to make seven triple-leaf groups. Glue the ends of two leaves together to make seven double-leaf groups, using the template as a guide.

4 Make seven berries. For each berry, roll 8-inch (20.3 cm) lengths of red quilling paper into tight circles. Glue a berry between the leaves of the double-leaf groups.

5 With the pencil and the cookie cutter, trace a circle on the center of the light-brown card stock.

6 Use the pencil to sketch the word *believe* or any holiday-themed phrase of your choice in the center of the circle. Trace over the pencil with the black felt-tip pen.

7 Glue the leaves and berries around the circle, alternating between the triple- and double-leaf groups, using the template as a guide.

Triple-leaf group

Double-leaf group
with berry

Manger
CARD

The reason for the Christmas season is to remember the birth of Jesus Christ. Celebrate by creating this beautiful card to share with family and friends.

REASON FOR THE SEASON

easy

4" × 10"
(10.2 × 25.4 cm)

What You Need

Basic Quilling Tool Kit (page 10)

Card stock: black, white

Quilling paper, ⅛ inch (3 mm) wide:
white, metallic gold, light brown,
pale peach

Template

Ink pad: gold

Crimper

Pencil

Computer-generated
or handwritten text

Quilling Shapes

star   *half circle*   *tight circle*

Technique

Crimping (page 18)

Circle Templates

Size 1   Size 2

Size 3   Size 6

What You Do

1 Cut out a 4 × 10-inch (10.2 × 25.4 cm) rectangle from black card stock. Score the middle of the card vertically and fold it in half.

2 Make nine white stars. For each one, roll a 4-inch (10.2 cm) length of white quilling paper into a star (CTB size 6) and press the sides inward to create four points. Glue the stars to the top half of the card.

3 Make the central star. Roll a 12-inch (30.5 cm) length of yellow quilling paper into a star (CTB size 2) and press the sides inward to create a raised point. Brush the top surface of the star with the gold ink.

4 Make the four rays of light. For each ray, cut 6-inch (15.2 cm) lengths of gold quilling paper and run it through the crimper. Trim two strips of paper into 3-inch (7.6 cm) lengths and the other two strips into 2½-inch (6.4 cm) lengths. With the pencil, lightly sketch four lines that branch out from a single point on the center of the top half of the card. Using the lines as your guide, glue the rays to the front of the card. Glue the star on top of the rays.

5 Make the manger. Roll a 16-inch (40.6 cm) length of light-brown quilling paper into a trapezoid shape. First, make a half circle and then pinch two more points on the curved part of the half circle (CTB size 1). For the manger's legs, trim two ¼-inch (6 mm) pieces of light-brown quilling paper and fold each piece in half crosswise. Glue the legs to the manger.

6 Make Baby Jesus. For the body, roll an 8-inch (20.3 cm) length of white quilling paper into a half circle (CTB size 3). For the head, roll a 16-inch (40.6 cm) length of pale peach into a tight circle. For the halo, roll a 1-inch (2.5 cm) length of gold into an oval-shaped loop.

7 Glue the manger and the baby's body, head, and halo onto the front of the card.

8 Use a computer to print *Reason for the Season* and *For unto us a child is born, unto us a Son is given* (or phrases of your choice) on white card stock. Trim the excess paper and glue *Reason for the Season* on the front of the card and *For unto us a child . . .* inside the card.

Manger

Central star

White star

Santa Hat & Mittens

GIFT TAGS

Decorate a gift package with a hat and a pair of warm mittens. These quilled tags will definitely warm the heart of the receiver!

easy

1½" × 3"
(3.8 × 7.6 cm)

What You Need

Basic Quilling Tool Kit (page 10)

Precut gift tags: light brown

Ink pad: green, red

Quilling paper, ⅛ inch (3 mm) wide:
white, crimson

Template

Cord: silver

Quilling Shapes

loose circle   *triangle*   *square*

half circle   *teardrop*   *rectangle*

Technique

Attaching End-to-End (page 15)

Circle Templates

Size 2   Size 3

Size 5   Size 6

What You Do

1. Ink the edge of one tag with green ink. Ink the edge of the other tag with red ink.

2. Make the Santa hat. For the pom-pom, roll a 2-inch (5.1 cm) length of white quilling paper into a loose circle. For the middle of the hat, roll a 12-inch (30.5 cm) length of crimson quilling paper into a triangle with a single curved point (CTB size 2). For the base of the hat, use the end-to-end technique to glue a 1-inch (2.5 cm) length of crimson to a 4-inch (10.2 cm) length of white. Starting from the white end, roll the strip into a square (CTB size 6); repeat to make three squares. Glue the squares together to form the hat's base and let it dry. Glue the middle of the hat, the hat's base, and the pom-pom together.

3. Make the mittens. For the palm, roll an 8-inch (20.3 cm) length of crimson quilling paper into a half circle (CTB size 3). For the thumb, roll a 2-inch (5.1 cm) length of crimson quilling paper into a teardrop. For the cuff, roll a 6-inch (15.2 cm) length of white into a rectangle (CTB size 5). Glue the pieces together to make the left-handed mitten. Repeat to make the right-handed mitten.

4. Glue the Santa hat and mittens onto the top of the tags.

5. Thread silver cording through the holes of the tags to attach to your gifts.

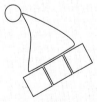

Hat

Mittens

Dove
CARD

Try your hand at a few quilling techniques with this easy holiday card. The design shows a simple decorative border with a graceful dove wishing peace and good will to all.

easy

4" × 11"
(10.2 × 27.9 cm)

What You Need

Basic Quilling Tool Kit (page 10)

Card stock: light brown, white,
sage green

Quilling paper, ⅛ inch (3 mm) wide:
metallic gold, white, sage green

Quilling paper, ¼ inch (6 mm) wide:
metallic gold

Template

Rub-on letters: gold
(or stamps and gold ink)

Quilling Shapes

teardrop   *arrow*   *loose circle*

marquise   *double
scroll*

Techniques

Banding (page 23)

Cutting Narrow Strips (page 24)

Circle Templates

Size 1   Size 2

Size 5

What You Do

1 Cut out a 4 × 11-inch (10.2 × 27.9 cm) rectangle from the light-brown card stock. Score the middle of the card vertically and fold it in half.

2 Cut out a 1 × 3¾-inch (2.5 × 9.5 cm) rectangle from the white card stock, and write *PEACE* on it using rub-on letters or stamps. Cut a piece of sage-green card stock slightly larger than the white piece and glue them together. Mount this to the front of the card.

3 Make the top and bottom gold borders. For each border, use the banding technique to wrap a 16-inch (40.6 cm) length of ⅛-inch-wide (3 mm) gold quilling paper around a 16-inch (40.6 cm) length of ¼-inch-wide (6 mm) gold quilling paper. Trim the edges so that they fit across the front of the card. Glue a gold border to the top and bottom of the front of the card.

4 Make the dove. For the body, roll a 16-inch (40.6 cm) length of white quilling paper into a teardrop (CTB size 1). For the tail, roll a 12-inch (30.5 cm) length of white quilling paper into an arrow (CTB size 2). For the head, roll a 6-inch (15.2 cm) length of white quilling paper into a loose circle and pinch a small point for the beak (CTD size 5). For the wings, cut a 12-inch (30.5 cm) length of white quilling paper in half lengthwise into a narrow ¹⁄₁₆-inch-wide (1.6 mm) strip to make two narrow strips. Roll each narrow strip into a teardrop (CTB size 2). Glue the head, body, tail, and wings together, using the template as reference. Let it dry. Then glue the completed dove to the front of the card.

5 Make the olive branch. Roll three 3-inch (7.6 cm) lengths of sage-green quilling paper into three marquises. Trim a small ½-inch (1.3 cm) strip of sage-green paper and glue it to the dove's beak. Glue the marquise leaves to the olive branch.

6 Make two leaf motifs. For each leaf motif, fold an 8-inch (20.3 cm) length of ⅛-inch (3 mm) gold quilling paper in half crosswise and roll into a double scroll. For the leaf, roll a 6-inch (15.2 cm) length of ⅛-inch (3 mm) gold quilling paper into a marquise (CTB size 5) and glue it to the double scroll as shown in the template. Repeat to make the other leaf motif. Glue the completed motifs on both sides of the word *PEACE*.

Dove and olive branch

Leaf motif

Silver Flower

GIFT TOPPER

Add a very special touch to your gifts by topping them with a floral bow.

easy

5" × 2¾"
(12.7 × 7 cm)

What You Need

Basic Quilling Tool Kit (page 10)

Quilling paper, ⅛ inch (3 mm) wide:
metallic silver, white

Border Buddy

Ink pad: silver

Template

Quilling paper, ¼ inch (6 mm) wide:
metallic silver

Quilling Shapes

marquise

loose cirle

Techniques

Border (page 17)

Beehive Swirls (page 18)

Gluing Back Sides
for a Freestanding Piece (page 21)

Circle Template

Size 5

What You Do

1. Make 12 circular borders. For each one, wrap a 16-inch (40.6 cm) length of ⅛-inch-wide (3 mm) silver quilling paper around the Border Buddy (size 3).

2. Make 12 beehive strips. For each strip, curl a 16-inch (40.6 cm) length of ⅛-inch-wide (3 mm) silver quilling paper and use the beehive technique along the entire paper strip.

3. Make 12 petals. For each petal, insert one beehive strip inside a circular border. Pinch the border into a marquise shape. Some of the beehive curls will be flattened. Spread glue on the back of each marquise petal. Ink the top edge of the petals with silver ink.

4. To make the bottom of the gift topper, glue six petals together.

5. Divide the remaining petals into three pairs. With the template as reference, glue the petals of each pair together.

6. Glue one pair of petals at an upward angle. Hold the petals in place for a few minutes to let the glue set. Repeat for the remaining pairs. Let the flower dry overnight.

7. For the center of the flower, roll a 6-inch (15.2 cm) length of white quilling paper into a loose circle (CTB size 5). Glue it to the center of the top petals.

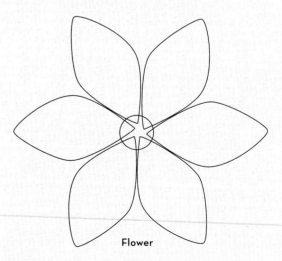

Flower

8 Make two silver ribbons. For each side, cut three 2-inch (5.1 cm) lengths of ¼-inch-wide (6 mm) silver quilling paper. Glue the three strips together at one end, each at a slight angle. Cut a V-shaped groove into the ends of each paper strip. Repeat for the other side.

9 Make two white ribbons. For each side, cut three 1½-inch (3.8 cm) lengths of white quilling paper. Glue the three strips together at one end, each at a slight angle. Cut the other ends at an angle and then glue them on top of the silver ribbons, using the template as reference. Repeat for the other side.

10 Curl the ends of the ribbons and glue the ribbons beneath the flower.

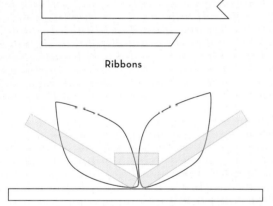

Ribbons

Side view of Silver Flower Gift Topper

Tip

Lay the border on a flat surface while pinching to prevent the coils from popping out.

Gingerbread House
CARD WITH
Gingerbread People
GIFT TAGS

This gingerbread house and people are a piece of cake!
Decorate them with quilled gumdrops and crimped icing.
Then share it with the cookie lover in your family!

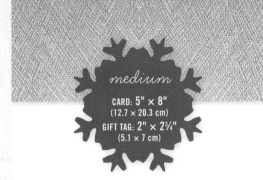

CARD: 5" × 8"
(12.7 × 20.3 cm)
GIFT TAG: 2" × 2¾"
(5.1 × 7 cm)

What You Need

Basic Quilling Tool Kit (page 10)

Card stock: light brown

Pencil

Quilling paper, ⅛ inch (3 mm) wide:
white, red, yellow, leaf green

Quillography paper, ⅛ inch (3 mm)
wide: white, leaf green

Template

Crimper

Ink pad: brown

Quilling Shapes

half circle   v-scroll   curved
                           teardrop

heart   tight circle   s-scroll

parallelogram

Techniques

Banding (page 23)

Cutting Narrow Strips (page 24)

Crimping (page 18)

Quillography (page 23)

What You Do
Gingerbread House Card

1 Cut out a 5 × 8-inch (12.7 × 20.3 cm) rectangle from the light-brown card stock. Score the middle of the card vertically and fold it in half.

2 Make the roof of the gingerbread house. With the pencil, mark a point at the center of the card's top edge, a point 1½ inches (3.8 cm) down from the top left corner of the card stock, and another point 1½ inches (3.8 cm) down from the top right corner of the card stock. Draw lines connecting the marked points using a ruler. With scissors or a craft knife, cut along the lines.

3 Make the candy cane trim along the left and right side of the card. For the trim on the left side, first roll an 8-inch (20.3 cm) length of white quilling paper into a half circle (CTB size 3). Next roll four 8-inch (20.3 cm) lengths of white quilling paper and four 8-inch (20.3 cm) lengths of red quilling paper into parallelograms (CTB size 3). Glue the white half circle on the bottom left corner of the card, as shown in the template. Then glue the parallelograms along the left side of the card, alternating between the red and white ones. Repeat for the trim on the right side of the card.

4 Make the snow on the roof. Roll eight 12-inch (30.5 cm) lengths of white quilling paper into teardrops (CTB size 2). Glue them along the roof of the card.

5 Make six gumdrops on the roof. For each gumdrop, roll a 6-inch (15.2 cm) length of quilling paper into a half circle (CTB size 5). You will make two red, two yellow, and two leaf-green gumdrops. Glue them on top of the snow, as shown in the template.

6 Make the two peppermint lollipops next to the door. For each lollipop, roll five 4-inch (10.2 cm) lengths of white quilling paper and five 4-inch (10.2 cm) lengths of red quilling paper into curved teardrops. Glue the 10 teardrops into a circle, alternating between the white and red pieces. Press the rounded end of the teardrops flat to give the candy a pinwheel pattern. Repeat for the other peppermint lollipop.

Circle Templates

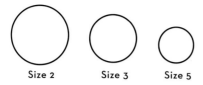

Size 2   Size 3   Size 5

7 Make the two sticks for the lollipops. For each stick, use a 6-inch (15.2 cm) length of white quillography paper and a 16-inch (40.6 cm) length of leaf-green quilling paper. Band the leaf green paper around the white quillography strip at a 45° angle. Trim the banded strip to the appropriate length. Glue the stick in place on the card and then glue the peppermint candy on top of the stick. Repeat for the other peppermint lollipop on the other side of the card. Save the rest of the banded strip for the windowsill.

8 Make the heart on the top of the card. Roll an 8-inch (20.3 cm) length of red quilling paper into a heart shape (CTB size 3). Glue it below the peak of the roof.

9 Make the two windows and the door. With the pencil, sketch the outline of the window and door, using the template as a reference. Cut a white 16-inch (40.6 cm) length of quillography paper in half lengthwise to form two narrow strips. Run the strips through the crimper. Using the quillography technique, glue the crimped quillography strips to create the windows and doors. Trim the strips using the template as a guide. Save the leftover crimped strips for making the door handle, decorative swirls surrounding the heart, and the gingerbread boy and girl.

10 Make the windowsill. Cut two 1-inch (2.5 cm) pieces from the leftover banded strip. Glue one piece onto the bottom edge of each window.

11 Make the door handle. Cut a 1-inch (2.5 cm) piece from the leftover crimped strips. Roll the piece into a tight circle. Glue it to the card.

12 Make the two decorative swirls on either side of the heart. For each swirl, cut a 1-inch (2.5 cm) piece from the leftover crimped strips. Roll the length into an S-scroll. Glue one swirl to the right of the heart and the other to the left.

13 Make the wreath on the door. Cut a 12-inch (30.5 cm) length of leaf-green quillography paper in half lengthwise to form two narrow strips. Run one strip through the crimper. Wrap the crimped strip around your finger to create the wreath. Glue the ends in place. Secure the wreath to the card inside the doorframe. For the wreath's bow and tails, cut a 4-inch (10.2 cm) length of red quilling paper in half lengthwise to form two narrow strips. Roll two 3-inch (7.6 cm) lengths of narrow red quilling paper into teardrops. Glue them on top of the wreath to form the bow. For the bow's tails, roll a 1-inch (2.5 cm) length of narrow red quilling paper into a V-scroll. Place the corner of the V-scroll below the center of the bow and glue it into place.

Gingerbread People Gift Tags

1. Using the template, trace the shapes of the gingerbread girl and boy onto the light-brown card stock.

2. Cut the shapes out and ink the edges with brown ink. Use the leftover crimped strip of white quillography paper as "icing" to decorate the boy and girl as you wish.

3. To use as gift tags, write the names of your recipients on the front and affix one to each gift with tape.

Leaping Deer
CARD

The outlined leaping deer in this card boldly
stands out from the quilled holly leaves.

4" × 5¼"
(10.2 × 13.3 cm)

What You Need

Basic Quilling Tool Kit (page 10)

Card stock: white, red

Pencil

Template

Quillography paper, ⅛ inch (3 mm) wide: white

Quilling paper, ⅛ inch (3 mm) wide: sage green, red

Quilling Shapes

holly leaf

loose circle

double scroll

Technique

Quillography (page 23)

Circle Template

Size 2

What You Do

1 Cut an 8 × 5¼-inch (20.3 × 13.3 cm) rectangle from the white card stock. Score the middle of the card horizontally and fold it in half. Cut a 3½ × 5-inch piece (8.9 × 12.7 cm) from the red card stock. Center and glue the red card stock to the front of the card.

2 With the pencil, trace the outline of the deer template onto the red card stock.

3 Using the quillography technique and the template, shape and glue the white quillography strips onto the outline. Trim the strips using the template as a guide.

4 Make two holly leaves. For each one, roll a 12-inch (30.5 cm) length of sage-green quilling paper into a holly leaf (CTB size 2).

5 Make six berries. For each berry, roll a 2-inch (5.1 cm) length of red quilling paper into a loose circle.

6 Make two double scrolls. Use a 4-inch (10.2 cm) length of sage-green quilling paper for each one.

7 Glue one scroll, one holly leaf, and three berries to the top left corner of the card. Glue the remaining scroll, holly leaf, and berries to the bottom right corner.

Holly leaves and berries

Deer

Santa Claus

CARD

Greet a special friend with "Ho, Ho, Ho."
Creating this jolly Santa will surely expand your quilling skills.

medium

4" × 5¼"
(10.2 × 13.3 cm)

What You Need

Basic Quilling Tool Kit (page 10)

Card stock: white, sage green

Pencil

Template

Quilling paper, ⅛ inch (3 mm) wide:
white, pale peach, pale pink, black, red

Round cookie cutter, 2 inches (5.1 cm)

Crimper

Quillography paper, ⅛ inch (3 mm) wide:
white

Quilling Shapes

crescent marquise tight oval

tight circle loose circle triangle

Techniques

Attaching End-to-End (page 15)

Multilayered Scroll (page 22)

Looping (page 16)

Cutting Narrow Strips (page 24)

Crimping (page 18)

Quillography (page 23)

Circle Templates

Size 1 Size 3 Size 6

What You Do

1 Cut out an 8 × 5¼-inch (20.3 × 13.3 cm) rectangle from the white card stock. Score the middle of the card vertically and fold it in half. Cut a 3½ × 4¼-inch piece (20.3 × 10.8 cm) from the sage-green card stock. Center and glue the sage-green card stock to the front of the card.

2 With the pencil and template, make the outline of the beard. Wrap a 16-inch (40.6 cm) length of white quilling paper around the cookie cutter to form a border. Bend and shape the circle using the template as a guide.

3 Make the mustache. Roll two 16-inch (40.6 cm) lengths of white quilling paper into crescents (CTB size 1). Glue the outline of the beard and the mustache to the lower half of the card.

4 Make eight beard curls. For each curl, glue the ends of three 2-inch (5.1 cm) lengths of white quilling paper together. Use the multilayered scroll technique to roll the strips. Glue the curls inside the beard.

5 Make four eight-looped pieces for the rim of the hat. For each piece, use a 16-inch (40.6 cm) length of white quilling paper and hand-loop the entire strip, using the template to determine its final length. Pinch to flatten and curve the loops. Glue them to the card as shown in the template.

6 Make the head. Roll fifteen 4-inch (10.2 cm) lengths of pale peach into marquises (CTB size 6). Glue them between the mustache and the rim of his hat.

7 Make the nose. Roll a 16-inch (40.6 cm) length of pale-pink quilling paper into a tight oval. Glue it on top of the mustache.

8 Make the two eyes. Cut a 2-inch (5.1 cm) length of black quilling paper in half lengthwise to make two narrow strips. Roll each narrow strip into a tight circle and glue them on the head.

9 Make the red hat. Roll fifteen 8-inch (20.3 cm) lengths of red quilling paper into loose circles (CTB size 3). Pinch the circles into ten marquises, four crescents, and one triangle. Using the template as reference, glue the pieces to the front of the card.

10 Make the hat's pom-pom. Run an 8-inch (20.3 cm) length of white quilling paper through the crimper. Gently roll the strip into a loose circle. Glue it to the end of the hat.

11 Using the quillography technique, trim or curl small pieces of white quillography strips to form three *Hs* and three *Os*. Glue *HO HO HO* next to Santa's head.

Eight-looped piece for the hat's rim (not shown to scale)

Pinecones
CARD

Bypass traditional colors this holiday and design a rustic card for that nature lover on your list. Use shades of brown quilling paper and layer the pieces to create a strikingly realistic pinecone.

Seasons Greetings

hard

7" × 5"
(17.8 × 12.7 cm)

What You Need

Basic Quilling Tool Kit (page 10)

Card stock: light blue, dark blue, sage green, white

Computer-generated text on white card stock, or black pen

Quilling paper, ⅛ inch (3 mm) wide: beige, light brown, brown, sage green, forest green

Template

Quilling Shapes

loose circle   *star*   *teardrop*
                 (variation)

Technique

Looping (page 16)

Circle Templates

Size 5   Size 6

What You Do

1 Cut out a 7 × 10-inch (17.8 × 25.4 cm) rectangle from the light-blue card stock. Score the middle of the card horizontally and fold it in half. Cut out a 6¾ × 9¾-inch (17.1 × 24.8 cm) rectangle from the dark-blue card stock. Center and glue it to the card. Cut a 6½ × 9½-inch (16.5 × 24.1 cm) rectangle from the sage-green card stock. Center and glue it to the card.

2 Cut out a 6¼ × 9¼-inch (15.9 × 23.5 cm) rectangle from the white card stock. Use a computer to print or a black pen to hand-write *Seasons Greetings* onto the white rectangle. Center and glue the white rectangle to the front of the card.

3 Make four large pinecone scales. For each large scale, roll a 6-inch (15.2 cm) length of beige quilling paper, a 6-inch (15.2 cm) length of light-brown quilling paper, and a 6-inch (15.2 cm) length of brown quilling paper into loose circles (CTB size 5). Pinch the beige circle into a star with two sides curved inward. Pinch the light-brown and brown coils into teardrops. Glue the three pieces together, using the template as a reference.

4 Make 14 small pinecone scales. For each small scale, roll a 4-inch (10.2 cm) length of beige quilling paper, a 4-inch (10.2 cm) length of light-brown quilling paper, and a 4-inch (10.2 cm) length of brown quilling paper into loose circles (CTB size 6). Pinch the beige coil into a star with two sides curved inward. Pinch the light-brown and brown coils into teardrops. Glue the three pieces together, using the template as a reference.

5 Assemble a pinecone. Lay out the large and small scales using the template, right, as a guide. Glue the scales together.

6 Repeat steps 3–5 to make the second pinecone.

7 Make two large sprigs and one small sprig. For each large sprig, fold a 16-inch (40.6 cm) length of sage-green quilling paper in half using the folding pine needles technique. For the small sprig, fold an 8-inch (20.4 cm) length of sage-green quilling paper in half using the folding pine needles technique, right.

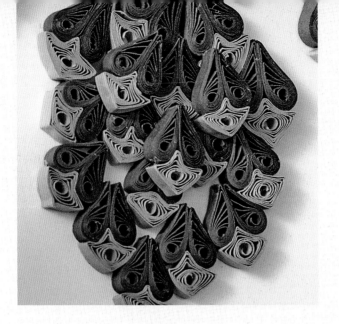

8 Repeat step 7 using the forest-green quilling paper.

9 Make three branches. For each branch, hand-loop a 16-inch (40.6 cm) length of brown quilling paper into a flat looped piece. Bend and crease the looped piece.

10 Glue the pinecones, sprigs of pine needles, and branches to the front of the card.

Pinecone

Pieces in gray are on a separate layer.
Large scale leaves are in blue.

Pine needle (top view)

Example of how to make the folds (not to scale)

Folding Pine Needles

1 Fold the strip in half crosswise. Make ½-inch-long (1.3 cm) zigzag folds along the length of each half of the strip, using the example in the template as a guide (**a**).

2 Starting on one side, place a small dab of glue on the inside of the folds and press them together to create the individual pine needles (**b**).

3 Repeat for the other side of the folded strip (**c**).

4 Glue both sides of the strip together (**d**).

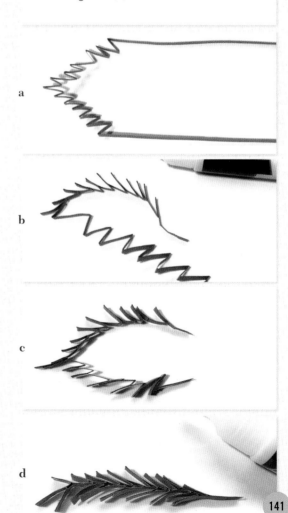

Acknowledgments

To Sterling Publishing, your creative staff is amazing, and I'm grateful for each opportunity to write a book with your team. To my family, who had to endure another season of me hiding in my office until the very late hours of the night. Thank you to my daughters, Rachel and Kayla, who patiently listened to me talk about Christmas ideas in July. Thank you to my husband, Dave, for cheering me on and cooking so many great dinners. Thank you, God, for blessing me with a wonderful life and the love of Jesus Christ in our home.

About the Author

Alli Bartkowski has been on the forefront of the quilling industry with her creative kits and innovative tools. Many of her ideas and products inspire others to learn and see beyond simple strips of paper. Her company, Quilled Creations, Inc. (quilledcreations.com), sells quilling supplies and has become the largest quilling company in the world. Alli is a member of the Craft and Hobby Association and an accredited member of the North American Quilling Guild. Her projects are featured in CardMaker magazine and on Quilled Creations, Inc.'s website. Alli is the author of *Quilled Mandalas*, *Quilled Flowers*, *Paper Quilling for the First Time*, *50 Nifty Quilled Cards*, and *Paper Quilling Kit for Dummies*. She continues to teach and share the art of quilling around the world!

Resources

Quilled Creations, Inc.
quilledcreations.com
tools, papers, quillography strips, highlight papers

Michaels
michaels.com
pennants, cording, ink pads, tea lights, tags, card stock, frames

Joann's Fabric & Craft Store
joann.com
jewelry findings, card stock, rhinestones, frames

Index